Explorer Encyclopedia

Edited by Bill Bruce

Contributors:
Michael Chinery
Christopher Maynard
Ian Ridpath
Jonathan Rutland

FRANKLIN WATTS
London

Published by Franklin Watts Ltd,
8 Cork Street, London W1
First published 1981

Designed and produced by Grisewood
& Dempsey Ltd, 20–22 Great Titchfield Street,
London W1

Printed and bound by Graficas Reunidas S.A.,
Madrid, Spain

SBN 85166 940 9

Contents

The Universe

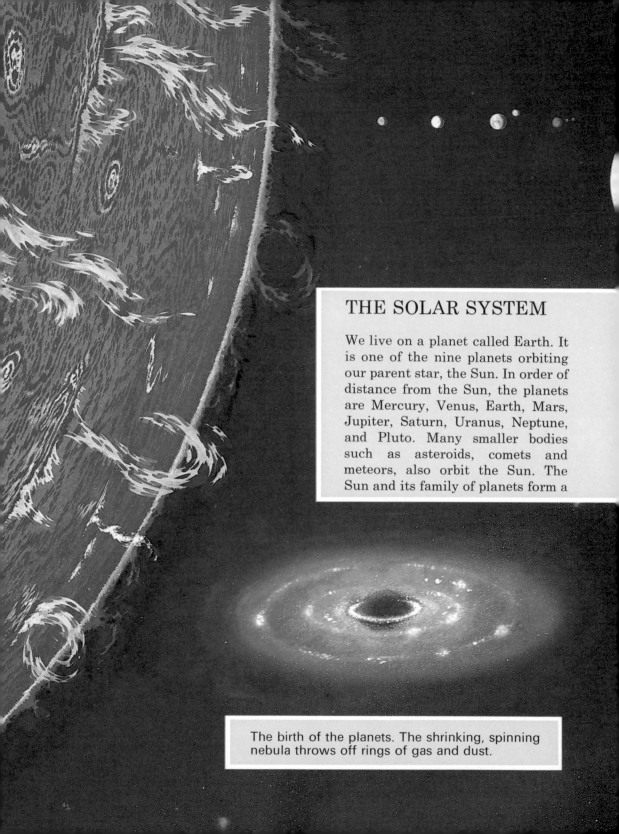

THE SOLAR SYSTEM

We live on a planet called Earth. It is one of the nine planets orbiting our parent star, the Sun. In order of distance from the Sun, the planets are Mercury, Venus, Earth, Mars, Jupiter, Saturn, Uranus, Neptune, and Pluto. Many smaller bodies such as asteroids, comets and meteors, also orbit the Sun. The Sun and its family of planets form a

The birth of the planets. The shrinking, spinning nebula throws off rings of gas and dust.

FACTS AND FIGURES ABOUT THE PLANETS

	Average Distance from Sun	Diameter	Length of Year	Moons
Mercury	58,000,000 km	4,870 km	88 Earth days	none
Venus	107,500,000 km	12,100 km	225 Earth days	none
Earth	150,000,000 km	12,742 km	365 Earth days	1
Mars	227,800,000 km	6,790 km	687 Earth days	2
Jupiter	780,420,000 km	142,500 km	11.9 Earth years	13
Saturn	1,431,000,000 km	120,000 km	29.1 Earth years	10
Uranus	2,877,000,000 km	49,000 km	84.0 Earth years	5
Neptune	4,486,000,000 km	50,000 km	164.8 Earth years	2
Pluto	5,930,000,000 km	3,000 km	248.0 Earth years	1

Gradually, the gas and dust form solid planets orbiting the Sun.

part of the Universe that we call the solar system.

The Sun

The Sun is a vast ball of gas 1.4 million km in diameter, over 100 times the width of the Earth. The Sun gives off heat and light which keeps us warm here on Earth. At the centre of the Sun is a 'powerhouse' of energy which keeps it glowing. Vast tongues of flame lick into space from the surface of the Sun, which has a temperature of 6,000°C.

Planets are much smaller and colder than the Sun, and they can be made from rock as well as gas.

The solar system is believed to have formed 4,700 million years ago from a giant cloud of gas and dust in space, known as a nebula. Under the inward pull of its own gravity, the nebula shrank. At its centre formed a glowing ball of gas—the Sun. Around the infant Sun, left-over rings of material from the nebula collected together into balls of rock and gas which became the planets.

The Earth

Our home planet, Earth, takes just over 365 days to orbit the Sun. We call this period of time a year. The Earth also continually spins on its axis like a top. It takes 24 hours to spin once, a period we call a day. The Earth's daily spin makes the Sun and other objects in the sky appear to rise and set. The other planets orbit the Sun, and spin on their axes, in different periods of time.

The Moon

The Earth has a natural satellite known as the Moon. The Moon is about a quarter the size of the Earth, large enough to be considered a mini-planet in its own right.

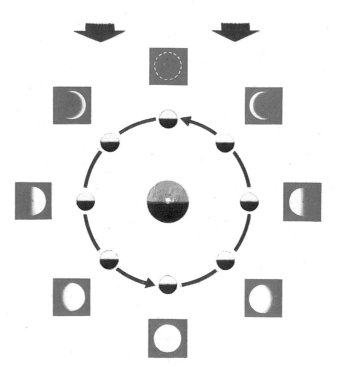

As the Moon orbits the Earth, it goes through a familiar cycle of phases, from new Moon (completely invisible), to full Moon, and back to new again.

Half the Moon is always illuminated by the Sun, but the Moon's phase depends on how much of that illuminated half is visible to us.

When the Moon is between the Sun and the Earth, all of the illuminated portion faces away from us and the Moon is invisible (new Moon). As the Moon moves around the Earth we at first see a thin crescent, then a half-illuminated Moon. When the Earth is between the Moon and the Sun, we see it fully illuminated (full Moon).

As the Moon moves from new to full it is said to be waxing. As it moves back to new Moon again it is said to be waning.

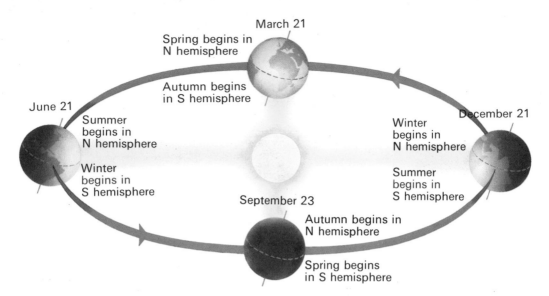

March 21
Spring begins in
N hemisphere

Autumn begins
in S hemisphere

June 21
Summer
begins in
N hemisphere

Winter
begins in
S hemisphere

December 21
Winter
begins in
N hemisphere

Summer
begins in
S hemisphere

September 23
Autumn begins in
N hemisphere

Spring begins
in S hemisphere

The Moon is a barren, airless ball of rock lying 385,000 km away from us. It orbits the Earth about every four weeks—a period of time known as a month.

Through telescopes we can see that the surface of the Moon is pockmarked with large depressions known as craters, up to 300 km across. In addition, there are dark lowland areas known as 'seas', even though there is no water on the Moon. The largest seas are more than 1,000 km across. These large, dark seas are just visible to the naked eye. Astronomers believe that the Moon's craters and seas were formed by meteorites and asteroids (stray lumps of rock and metal in the solar system) which blasted into the lunar surface. The biggest depressions were later flooded by molten lava from inside the Moon, which has long since cooled and solidified to form the dark low seas.

What are the other planets of the solar system like? Investigation by telescope and space probe has told us a lot about Earth's neighbouring worlds.

Mercury
The closest planet to the Sun is Mercury.

On most of the Earth, the temperature changes season by season. It changes because the Earth's axis is tilted in space in relation to the path it follows around the Sun. Because of this, a particular spot on Earth is angled more towards the Sun, and is hotter at some times of the year than at others. Places in the northern hemisphere are angled towards the Sun on about June 21 each year. This is their longest day and midsummer. Places in the southern hemisphere are angled away from the Sun on that date. This is their shortest day.

It is an airless, waterless, rocky ball only 50 per cent larger than our own Moon. Pictures from the Mariner 10 space probe have shown that Mercury looks like the Moon—its surface is pitted with craters and lava plains. From Mercury, the Sun would appear $2\frac{1}{2}$ times larger in the sky than it does from Earth. Because Mercury is so close to the Sun, temperatures on its day side reach 400°C, hot enough to melt tin and lead. On the night side of Mercury, temperatures drop to a frigid −170°C. No one could live on Mercury.

Venus

The second planet from the Sun is Venus, which was once termed 'Earth's twin' because of its similarity in size with our own world. Venus can appear brighter in the sky than any other bodies except the Sun and Moon. This is because it comes closer to us than any other planet and it is covered in an unbroken blanket of clouds which reflect the Sun's light. These clouds are not like the clouds of Earth, which are made of water vapour. Instead, the clouds of Venus are made of strong sulphuric acid!

Venus has a dense atmosphere, but we could not breathe it. The atmosphere of Venus is made of carbon dioxide gas, which we would find poisonous. This dense atmosphere traps heat from the Sun like a blanket, forcing temperatures at the surface of the planet up to a furnace-like 475°C. Because of this intense heat, there are no seas on Venus—all the water has evaporated. Venus is far too hostile a planet for humans to live on.

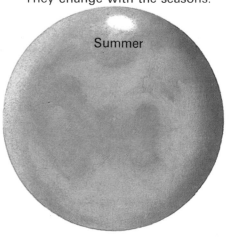

Mars has polar ice caps.
They change with the seasons.

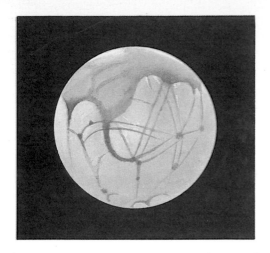

Some astronomers thought that they could see 'canals' on Mars and drew maps like this one. They wondered if there had once been a Martian civilization. Recent space probes have found no trace of 'canals' and no signs of life on the planet.

Like our Moon, Venus has 'phases'. It waxes (grows full) and wanes (becomes invisible). It is full when it is farthest away. As it approaches Earth, it looks bigger but less of it is lit by the Sun, so only a narrow crescent can be seen.

Mars

Beyond Earth, we come to the planet Mars, about half Earth's size. Mars is commonly known as the red planet, because of the colour of the sands that cover its surface. Mars has a thin atmosphere of carbon dioxide, and icy polar caps.

Although Mars is much colder than Earth, some scientists thought that simple vegetation might exist on the red planet. But the Viking space probes which landed on the surface in 1976 found no signs of life on Mars. But space probes have found giant volcanoes and an enormous canyon on Mars, so it would be an exciting planet to explore. One day, humans might set foot on Mars.

Mars has two tiny moons, called Phobos and Deimos. These are irregularly shaped lumps of rock, probably former asteroids which strayed too close to Mars and were captured by its gravity.

Most asteroids, of which over 2,000 are known, orbit in a belt between Mars and the next planet, Jupiter.

Jupiter

Jupiter is the largest planet in the solar system. It is a ball of swirling gas, 11 times the diameter of the Earth and weighing $2\frac{1}{2}$ times as much as all the other planets put together! Jupiter's clouds are drawn out into multi-coloured bands by the planet's swift rotation, once every 9 hours 50 minutes. Among the clouds is an enormous red spot, which is believed to be the top of a storm cloud in Jupiter's atmosphere.

Jupiter has at least 13 moons (more are suspected), the largest of which are bigger than our own Moon. The two Voyager space probes in 1979 showed that Jupiter's moons are little worlds in their own right, with craters, ice fields, and even volcanoes.

Saturn

Saturn (in the box on the right) is a very beautiful planet. It is encircled by bright rings, made of tiny fragments of rock coated with ice. Saturn has a family of at least 10 moons. The largest, Titan, has a dense atmosphere of its own.

Uranus and Neptune

Uranus and Neptune are planets made largely of gas. They are so far from the Sun they cannot be seen properly through telescopes, and no space probe has yet reached them. In 1977, a set of faint rings was discovered around Uranus. There may be rings around Neptune, too.

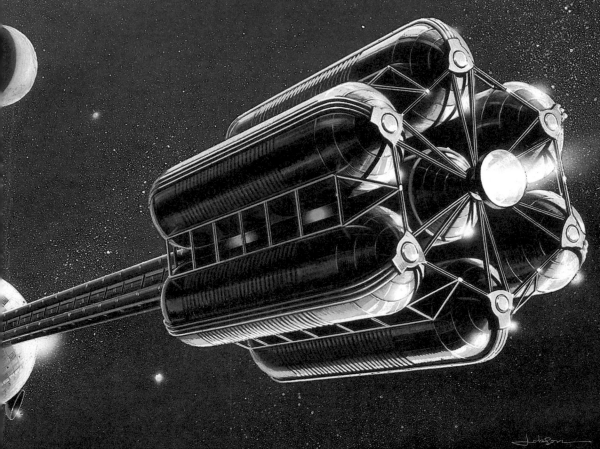

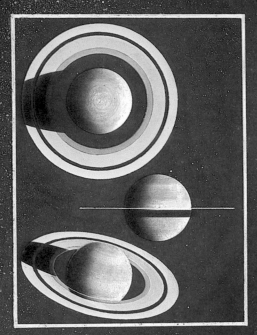

Pluto

At the edge of the solar system lies the smallest planet, Pluto. It is visible only as a star-like speck through telescopes. It was discovered when photographs of the same area of stars on different nights showed a 'wanderer' (arrowed in the picture on the far left). Pluto's orbit crosses that of Neptune, and from 1979 to 1999 Pluto actually lies closer to the Sun than Neptune.

Astronomers have found no planets beyond Pluto. Probably only a belt of comets exists beyond Pluto. Then there is nothing until the further stars.

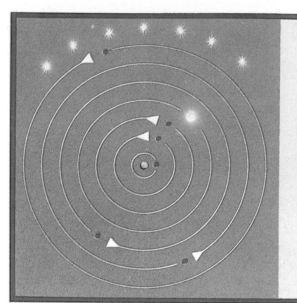

In ancient times, astronomers discovered five 'wandering stars' or planets. They named them after gods—Mercury, Venus, Mars, Jupiter, and Saturn. Ancient maps of the Universe, like the one shown here, put the Earth rather than the Sun at the centre. Moving around the Earth these maps showed the Moon, Mercury, Venus, the Sun, Mars, Jupiter and Saturn.

ASTRONOMY

Centuries ago, people believed that the Earth lay at the centre of the Universe, with everything else circling it. In 1543 a Polish monk, Nicolaus Copernicus, proposed a different theory—that the Sun was the centre of the Universe, and that the Earth was just an ordinary planet orbiting it. We now know that not even the Sun is the centre of the Universe. Instead, it is just one star in a galaxy of 100,000 million other stars, called the Milky Way. The Milky Way is only one galaxy among countless others spread throughout the Universe. At present, no one knows how the Universe began, but we do know many other things about it.

The First Telescopes
The invention of the telescope in the early 17th century was very important. One of the first people to turn a telescope towards the sky was the Italian scientist Galileo. He used a refractor telescope.

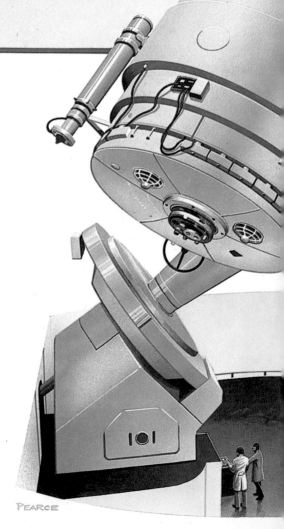

PEARCE

18

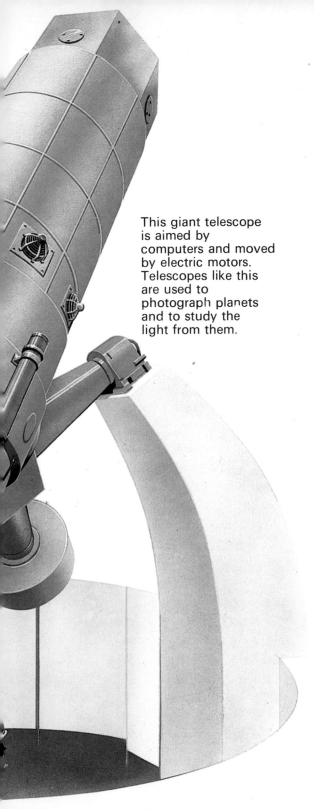

This giant telescope is aimed by computers and moved by electric motors. Telescopes like this are used to photograph planets and to study the light from them.

This design uses lenses to collect and focus light. Telescopes can show objects too faint to be seen with the naked eye, as well as magnifying them to make them appear larger. In 1668, Isaac Newton built the first of another type of telescope, known as a reflector. Reflectors use a mirror to collect and focus light. Most modern large telescopes are reflectors, because big mirrors are cheaper and easier to make than lenses.

The largest reflecting telescope, in the Soviet Union, has a mirror 6m in diameter. The second-largest reflector is that on Mount Palomar in California, with a mirror 5m in diameter. The largest refractor, at Yerkes Observatory in Wisconsin, USA, has a lens 1m in diameter.

Modern Telescopes

In recent years, astronomers have developed telescopes capable of detecting radio waves that are emitted naturally by objects in space. Radio telescopes, as they are called, are proving vital in studying the Universe. Radio telescopes can consist of one large dish-shaped aerial to collect radio waves, or they may be made up of a group of smaller aerials. The largest radio-telescope dish, 305m in diameter, is at Arecibo in Puerto Rico.

Astronomers are now using satellites and telescopes in space to study the Universe. Today's telescopes can detect objects so far away that their light has taken thousands of millions of years to reach us. The distance that light travels in one year is termed a light year (one light year equals about $9\frac{1}{2}$ million million km). The most distant objects visible in the Universe are about 15,000 million light years away. One day, we may even set up permanent observatories on the surface of the Moon.

LOOKING AT THE STARS

The star maps on this and the opposite page are of the northern and southern hemispheres looking north and south at 11.30 pm on the first days of January and July.

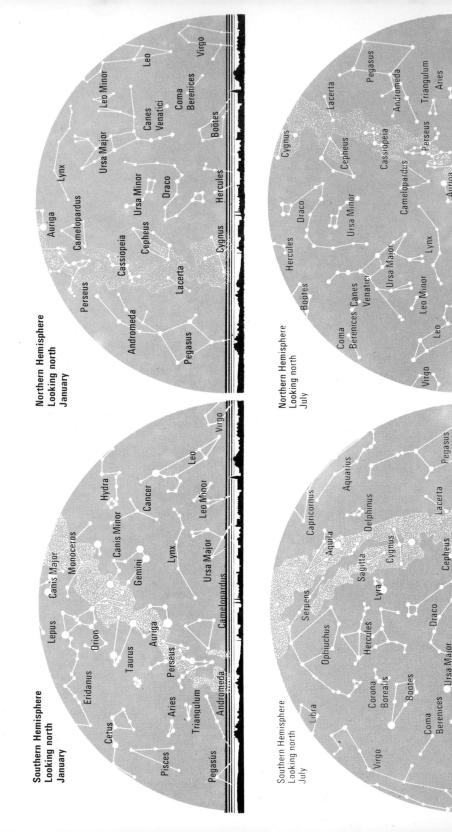

Southern Hemisphere
Looking north
January

Northern Hemisphere
Looking north
January

Southern Hemisphere
Looking north
July

Northern Hemisphere
Looking north
July

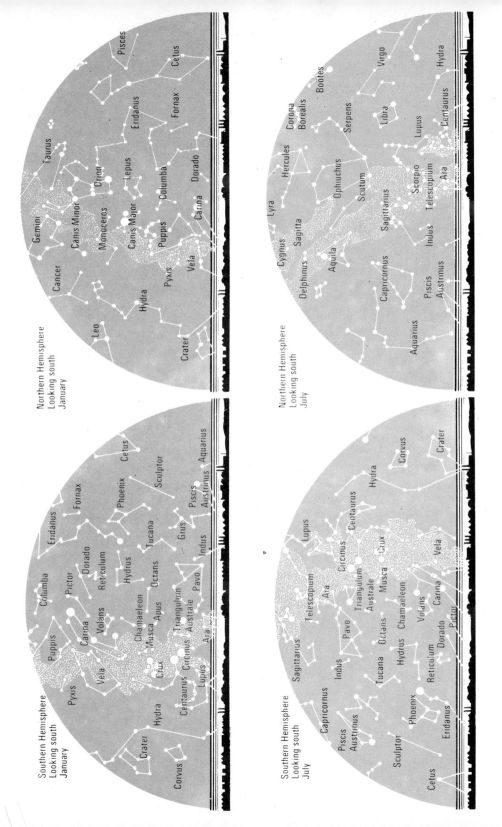

Northern Hemisphere
Looking south
January

Northern Hemisphere
Looking south
July

Southern Hemisphere
Looking south
January

Southern Hemisphere
Looking south
July

21

ESCAPE FROM EARTH

American astronaut Neil Armstrong was the first man to set foot on the Moon. He did so on July 21, 1969. Armstrong, and his colleagues Edwin Aldrin and Michael Collins, had blasted off five days before from Cape Canaveral, Florida, on top of a giant Saturn V rocket.

Rockets provide the power to break away from the pull of the Earth's gravity and get into space. The bigger the spacecraft to be launched, the larger the rocket that is needed. The Saturn V rocket design was built in three stages. The stages dropped away one at a time as they ran out of fuel.

A Saturn V rocket blasts-off from its launch pad. The American Saturn V, standing 111 metres high, was the biggest rocket ever built. It was used to take Apollo spacecraft to the Moon and also put the Skylab space station into orbit.

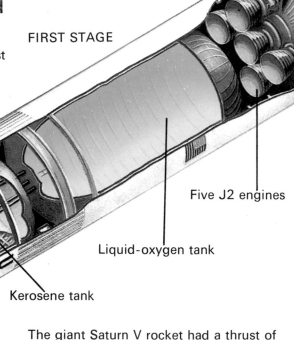

FIRST STAGE

Five F1 engines

Five J2 engines

Liquid-oxygen tank

Kerosene tank

Stabilizer

Fairing

The giant Saturn V rocket had a thrust of 3.5 million kg at lift-off. Each of its five powerful rocket motors burned over three tonnes of fuel each second to reach the escape velocity of 40,000 km/h.

22

The Apollo spacecraft sat on top of the mighty Saturn V rocket for its journey to the Moon. By the time it went into orbit around the Earth, the first stages of the rocket had fallen away.

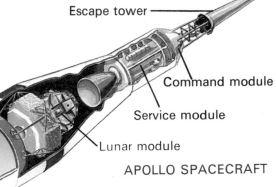

Escape tower

Command module

Service module

Lunar module

APOLLO SPACECRAFT

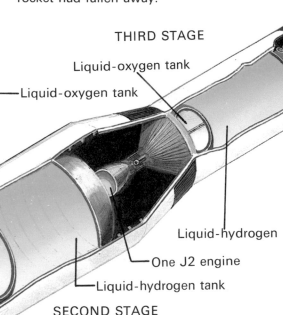

THIRD STAGE

Liquid-oxygen tank

Liquid-oxygen tank

Liquid-hydrogen

One J2 engine

Liquid-hydrogen tank

SECOND STAGE

As the rocket went into orbit, the Command and Service modules separated from the third stage and then turned to 'dock' with the Lunar module before heading for the Moon.

The three astronauts rode in an Apollo capsule at the top of the rocket. Underneath them was a craft called the lunar module, into which Armstrong and Aldrin crawled to make their lunar landing. They returned to Earth with samples of the Moon's surface for scientists to analyse. Other astronauts also went to the Moon before the Apollo programme finished in 1972.

The Space Age

The Space Age had begun on October 4, 1957, when a Russian rocket put the first artificial satellite, called Sputnik 1, into orbit around the Earth. Other Russian and American satellites followed, and by

1980, about 2,000 satellites and probes had been launched. Some of the most important satellites are used for communications, weather forecasting and navigation.

People in Space

The first man to fly in space was a Russian, Yuri Gagarin, who orbited the Earth once on April 12, 1961. He flew in a spherical spacecraft called Vostok. Other Russians orbited the Earth in Vostok spacecraft, including the first spacewoman, Valentina Tereshkova. In March 1965, two Soviet cosmonauts flew together in a spacecraft called Voskhod. One of the men, Alexei Leonov, crawled out of the capsule in a spacesuit to make the first 'walk' in space.

The first American astronauts flew in a conical single seat spacecraft called Mercury. Then, in 1965 and 1966, came the series of two-man Gemini flights. Astronauts practised meeting and docking with other craft in space, in preparation for the Apollo Moon flights.

The Apollo Programme

The Apollo spacecraft consisted of a conical crew compartment 3.9 metres across, called the command module, in which the three astronauts rode. Behind this was a cylindrical section, the service module, which contained fuel and supplies as well as a large engine for manoeuvring in space. The lunar module was a separate, spidery craft which actually touched down on the Moon. On later landings the astronauts used an electrically powered Moon buggy.

Space Stations

Apollo capsules were also used to ferry crews up to the Skylab space station, launched in 1973. Skylab, made from the converted top stage of a Saturn V rocket, was the largest object ever put into space. It measured 25 metres long and weighed 75 tonnes. Three crews lived and worked in Skylab for up to three months at a time before it was abandoned.

The Soviet Union has launched a series of space stations called Salyut. Cosmonauts fly up to Salyut aboard Soyuz spacecraft. In 1979, cosmonauts Vladimir Lyakhov and Valery Ryumin spent a record of nearly six months aboard a Salyut space station. Doctors believe that humans can survive in space for very long

Apollo Command and Service Module

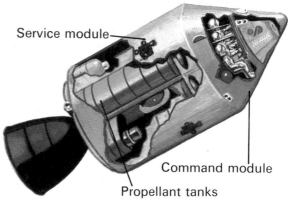

Service module

Command module

Propellant tanks

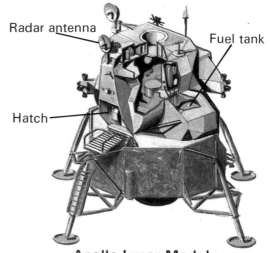

Radar antenna

Fuel tank

Hatch

Apollo Lunar Module

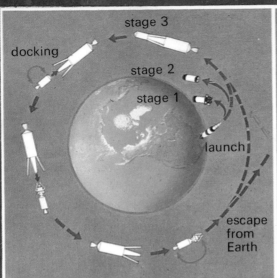

stage 3

docking

stage 2

stage 1

launch

escape from Earth

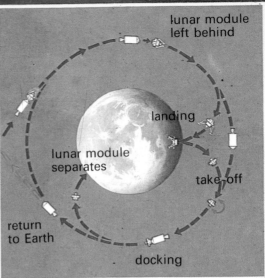

lunar module left behind

landing

lunar module separates

take-off

return to Earth

docking

UNITED STATES

1

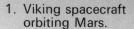

2

3

periods—perhaps for a year or more at a time, long enough for a flight to Mars. In the future, much larger space stations, capable of holding dozens of people, may be set up.

Space Probes

Before men go to the planets, robot explorers called space probes are paving the way. The first probes were sent to the Moon, but now all the planets out to Saturn have been visited and photographed by probes. The first successful probe to another planet was the American Mariner 2, which reached Venus in 1962. Other Mariners have examined Mercury and Mars, revealing craters and other details on their surfaces. Soviet probes have parachuted to the surface of Venus to study conditions there.

One of the most exciting planetary probes was Viking. This landed on Mars in 1976 to look for life, although it did not find any. Spectacular colour pictures of the swirling clouds of Jupiter were sent back in 1979 by two Voyager spacecraft. The Voyagers then headed for Saturn, reaching there in 1980. One Voyager is scheduled to fly on to Uranus, which it will reach in 1986. It may continue to Neptune, which it would reach in 1989.

In future, probes may be used to bring back samples of soil from Mars automatically. Other probes are planned to fly near comets, which are ghostly bags of rock and dust that wander throughout the solar system.

1. Viking spacecraft orbiting Mars.
2. Lander module separates from orbiter.
3. The parachute opens, the aeroshell is jettisoned and the lander's legs are extended.
4. Retro-rockets fire for a gentle touchdown.
5. The Viking craft landed in 1976.

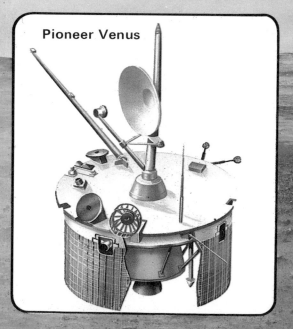

Pioneer Venus

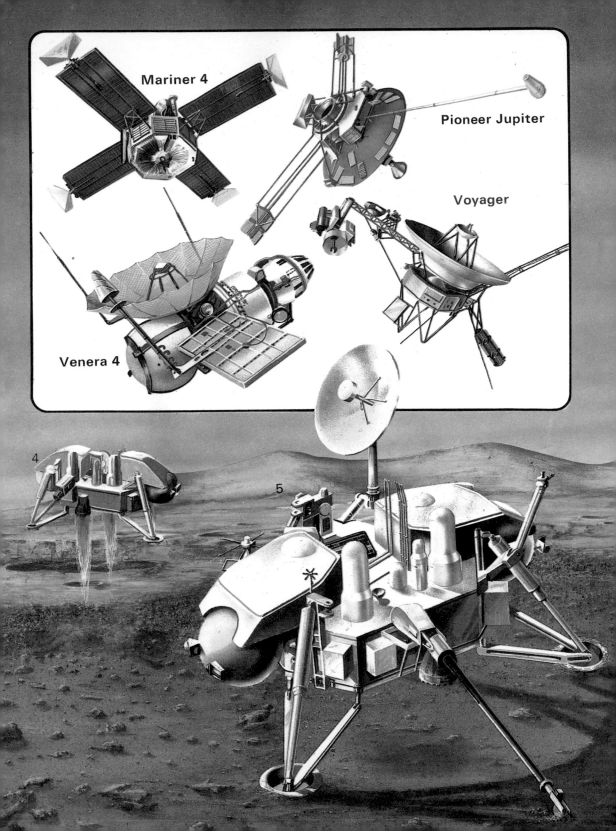

Mariner 4

Pioneer Jupiter

Voyager

Venera 4

4

5

3

4.

THE NEW AGE

2

Ordinary rockets are thrown away each time, so that a new rocket has to be built for each space launch. This is very wasteful. The Space Shuttle is a reusable space plane which makes space-flight much cheaper.

The Space Shuttle orbiter is a winged craft 37.2 m long, the size of a large jet plane, with a cargo bay capable of carrying 29 tonnes. As in an aircraft, the pilots sit in the nose. At its launch, the Shuttle orbiter is joined to a large fuel tank which feeds its engines. Two other rockets are added at the sides to assist take-off. As the Shuttle climbs, these side rockets fall away and are recovered. Once the Shuttle reaches orbit, the large fuel tank also falls away.

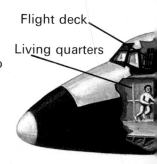

Flight deck

Living quarters

The Shuttle orbiter, cut away to show the space laboratory, Spacelab, which it will carry into space. Inside the pressurized module, teams of scientists and engineers will work for up to a month.

1

5

6

The Shuttle can carry several satellites into space at once, and it can also bring back unwanted or malfunctioning satellites from orbit. To return to Earth, the winged orbiter glides down through the atmosphere and lands on a runway like an aircraft. It is then made ready for launch again.

An important load that the Shuttle will carry is Spacelab, a space station built by the European Space Agency. Spacelab will ride in the Shuttle's cargo bay for a week at a time, while men and women scientists from the United States and Europe work in space, conducting research and experiments, and observing the Earth and sky.

One day, it may be possible to take holidays in space aboard the Shuttle!

1. Shuttle take-off. Side boosters and main engines fire together.
2. Their fuel used up, the boosters separate and parachute back to Earth.
3. Main tank separates.
4. Shuttle orbiter carries out operations in orbit.
5. After its mission the orbiter drops from orbit and re-enters the atmosphere.
6. With landing wheels down, the orbiter glides to a touchdown on the runway.

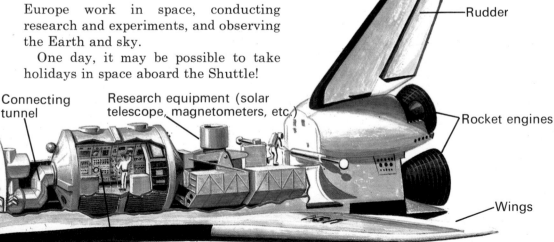

Rudder

Connecting tunnel

Research equipment (solar telescope, magnetometers, etc.)

Rocket engines

Wings

Laboratory

COUNTRIES IN SPACE

1. USSR — 1957 *Sputnik 1*
2. USA — 1958 *Explorer 1*
3. Canada — 1962 *Alouette 1*
4. Italy — 1964 *San Marco 1*
5. France — 1965 *A-1 (Astérix)*
6. Great Britain — 1967 *Ariel 3*
7. Australia — 1967 *WRESAT 1*
8. West Germany — 1969 *Azur 1*
9. Japan — 1970 *Osumi 1*
10. China — 1970 *Chicom 1*
11. Netherlands — 1974 *NAS*
12. Spain — 1974 *Intasat*
13. India — 1975 *Arya Bhatta*

COMETS

	First seen	Orbital period (in years)
Halley's Comet	240 BC	76
Encke's Comet	1786	3.3
Biela's Comet	1806	6.7
Great Comet of 1811	1811	3,000
Pons-Winnecke	1819	6.0
Great Comet of 1843	1843	512.4
Donati's Comet	1858	2,040
Schwassmann-Wachmann Comet	1925	16.2
Arend-Roland Comet	1957	10,000
Humason Comet	1961	2,900
Ikeya-Seki Comet	1965	880

MAN ON THE MOON

Names and Dates	Code Name	Achievements	Crew
Apollo 11 July 1969	Columbia (CM) Eagle (LM)	First landing on Moon. First moonwalk for 2½ hours. 22 hours spent on moon.	Neil Armstrong Edwin Aldrin Michael Collins
Apollo 12 November 1969	Yankee Clipper (CM) Intrepid (LM)	Second moonlanding. 31 hours spent on Moon.	Charles Conrad Alan Bean Richard Gordon
Apollo 13 April 1970	Odyssey (CM) Aquarius (LM)	Explosion in service module caused mission abort. Crew returned safely.	James Lovell Fred Haise John Swigert
Apollo 14 February 1971	Kitty Hawk (CM) Antares (LM)	Third landing. 33½ hours on Moon. Two moonwalks totalled nine hours.	Alan Shepard Edgar Mitchell Stuart Roosa
Apollo 15 July–August 1971	Endeavour (CM) Falcon (LM)	Fourth landing. Three days on Moon. Lunar roving vehicle made three trips.	David Scott James Irwin Alfred Worden
Apollo 16 April 1972	Casper (CM) Orion (LM)	Fifth landing. Three days on Moon. Three trips made by Lunar roving vehicle.	John Young Charles Duke Thomas Mattingly
Apollo 17 December 1972	Challenger (CM) America (LM)	Sixth landing. The end of the Apollo programme and the last landing on the Moon.	Eugene Cernan Harrison Schmitt Ronald Evans

Notes: Commander named first, Lunar Module pilot named second, Command Module pilot third.
(CM) – Command Module   (LM) – Lunar Module

The Earth

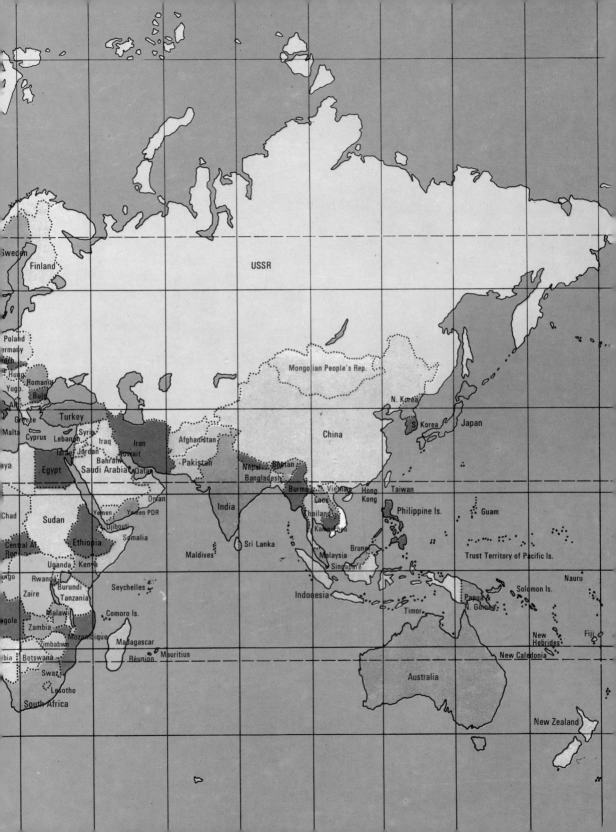

Below: How the continents
have drifted over millions of
years.

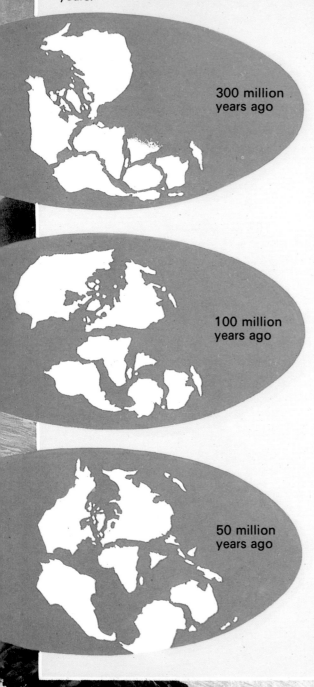

300 million
years ago

100 million
years ago

50 million
years ago

IN THE BEGINNING

The Earth is around 4,600 million years old. Nobody is certain how it began, but one theory is that it was formed from a ring of dust and gas, orbiting around the Sun. Over a period of millions of years the dust and gas was drawn together by gravity to form a solid ball. Enormous pressure and energy made the materials from which the new planet grew very hot. In the seething inferno, heavy substances sank down into the centre of the Earth, while lighter ones floated up. The heaviest materials were metals, and scientists think that the core of our planet consists mainly of iron and nickel. The core is still enormously hot. It probably consists of a solid inner core and a liquid outer core.

The lighter substances which floated up included gases like oxygen and hydrogen, and the elements from which rock is made. The elements combined in different ways to forms different kinds of rock. At first, all these rocks were so hot that they were molten, or liquid. Gases bubbled up through the molten rock and formed the beginnings of an atmosphere. At this stage, Earth was a hostile planet, far too hot for any form of life, or for water.

Slowly it began to cool down. This took millions of years, but eventually the rocks on the surface hardened to form a crust. This thin outer layer of solid rock floated on a much thicker layer of still molten rock called the mantle. In many places the crust was weak, and molten rock from beneath burst through. Such places are called volcanoes.

Today, molten rock still breaks through. Our planet is still changing. Even the continents we live on are moving. The crust still floats on the mantle. It is made up of gigantic plates like the pieces of a jigsaw puzzle. The plates drift around on the mantle, which is still almost liquid, like soft toffee.

Steam was one of the gases bubbling up through the young Earth's surface. At first, the planet was too hot for the steam to turn to water, but eventually the time came when the clouds of steam enveloping the world would turn to rain. The deluge that followed probably lasted for centuries, forming pools, then lakes and then the oceans. The large picture shows how the world may have looked when the oceans were being born.

THE OCEANS

Scientists think that at first there was just one ocean. It covered almost three quarters of the Earth's surface, and completely surrounded a single vast continent. The original continent has broken up to form many different land masses. This has happened because the 'plates' which form the Earth's crust have drifted apart. These plates are platforms on which the continents and the ocean floors float. They have been pushed about by movements in the molten rock. So today, the continents divide the original ocean into different oceans and seas.

The Pacific

By far the largest stretch of water is the Pacific Ocean. It covers more of the Earth's surface than all the land put together, and stretches half-way around the world, from Australia to America. The Pacific is also the deepest ocean, and the lowest spot on Earth is in the western Pacific. It is called the Marianas Trench and has a depth of 11,000 metres. It could easily drown the world's highest mountain.

The Atlantic

Next in size is the Atlantic Ocean, which separates Europe and Africa from the American continent. Beneath it are vital supplies of oil and gas.

The Indian

This is the third largest ocean. It separates Africa, Asia and Australia. On its borders lie two areas which are changing size because of movements of the plates. The Red Sea is getting slowly wider, pushing land into the Persian Gulf, which is getting smaller.

The Arctic and Antarctic

The southern regions of the Pacific, Atlantic and Indian oceans are sometimes known as the Antarctic or Southern Ocean. But the fourth main ocean is the Arctic Ocean. This lies to the north of Asia and North America. Much of it is covered by ice, and it lies in darkness half the year.

The Seas

Seas, bays and gulfs are smaller stretches of water lying around the edges of the oceans and continents. Gulfs and bays are partly enclosed by land, while seas are usually open water between land masses. All these stretches of water are linked together to form a single vast mass of water. However, there are two 'seas', the Dead Sea and the Caspian Sea, which are completely surrounded by land.

A Watery Landscape

Beneath the seas and oceans lies a landscape quite like that of the dry land. The sea bed is made up of mountains and valleys, ridges, plateaux and plains. Around the edges of the continents runs a sloping platform. This is called the continental shelf. Its shallow waters are rich in plant and animal life. Sometimes it stretches hundreds of kilometres out into the ocean before dropping sharply down to the main ocean floor. The main floor of the ocean is mostly about 3.5 kilometres deep. Here and there it plunges down into long gashes called trenches. Along the middle of most oceans mountain chains rise sharply.

The mid-ocean ridges and trenches are formed where plates in the Earth's crust meet. The trenches occur where one plate is being forced down underneath another. The ridges are great chains of volcanic mountains. Here, molten rock forces its

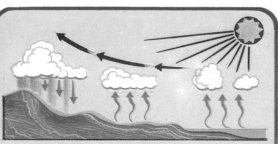

Atlantic

Pacific

Above: In hot sun, some of the seawater turns into water vapour. It evaporates and rises into the sky. As it rises it cools and condenses, forming tiny droplets. These make up clouds, which produce rain. The rain returns the water to the sea. This is called the water cycle. All the water in the world comes originally from the sea and all living things are made up largely of water.

Right: The two globes of the Atlantic and Pacific Oceans show clearly that most of the planet is covered by water.

At either side of this picture you can see the shallow continental shelves sloping gently down from the land before they plunge steeply down to the ocean floor. In the middle the mid-ocean ridge rises up, and in places projects above the water to form islands. To the left of the ridge is a trench.

way up along the joins between the plates. Sometimes the mountains rise so high that they stick up above the oceans.

Because of all this movement, the rocks of the sea bed are much younger than those on dry land. The oldest are only 200 million years old, compared to 3,800 million years for some rocks on land.

Sea Water

Sea water contains many substances including minute amounts of gold and other metals. The most common chemical in the water is salt, or sodium chloride. The salt and other materials are washed off the land by rain and rivers, and carried into the sea. This has been going on since the birth of the oceans, so the waters of the seas have been getting steadily more salty.

Below: The ocean currents of the world. Warm currents (shown pink) carry warm water to cold regions. Cold currents

In the Bay of Fundy in southeast Canada, the tide rises an amazing 15 metres. The catch in the fishermen's nets is left literally 'high and dry' as the tide recedes.

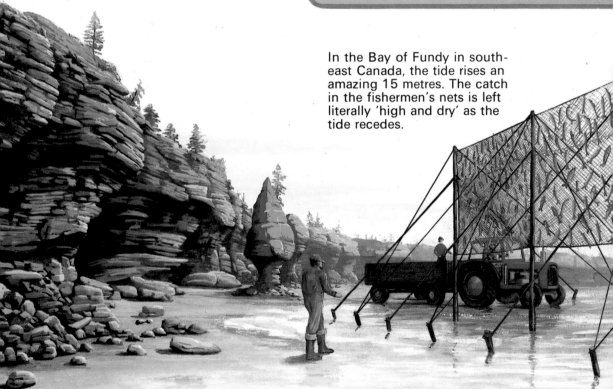

(shown blue) bring cold water to warm regions. In this way, the world's water is continually on the move.

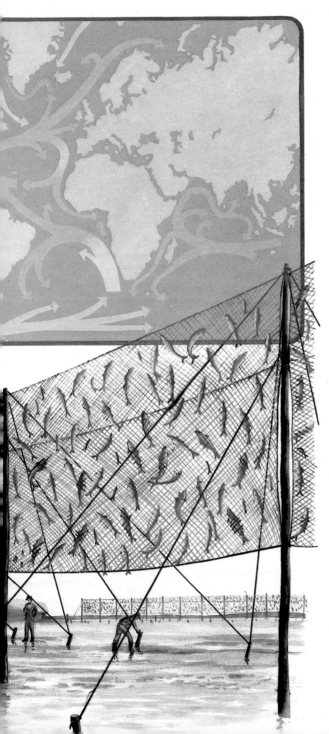

The seas are always moving, stirred by wind and waves, tides and currents. Strong winds whip up the surface waters into waves. During a storm, waves form that are higher than houses, and can wreck the largest ship. When large waves crash against the shore, they wear down the rock and may even break away great chunks of a cliff. This process is called erosion.

The Currents

There are two types of ocean currents—surface and deep sea. Deep sea currents are caused mainly by cold water at the North and South Poles sinking down and spreading out deep below the surface. Surface currents are formed by strong steady winds. The map shows the main currents.

Currents would simply circle around the globe if there were no land, but when they meet continents they are forced to change direction. North of the equator the currents of the Atlantic and Pacific sweep in great clockwise circles. South of the equator their direction is anticlockwise.

The Tides

Tides are the other force that move the waters of the oceans. They are caused by gravity between the Moon and the Earth, and the Sun and the Earth. The force of gravity pulls the water like a magnet and as the Earth spins, so the part of the oceans pulled most strongly changes. In each 24 hour period, two high and low tides sweep around the globe rather like giant waves. In the open sea, tides only raise the water by about one metre. Near land the difference is much greater. The highest tides occur when the Sun and Moon are in line and are pulling together.

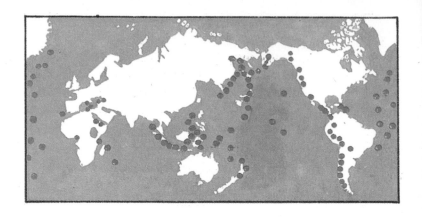

Most of the world's volcanoes occur in groups. There is a large group in Indonesia and there are volcanoes clustered around the Pacific Ocean like a 'ring of fire'. A third belt lies in the Atlantic Ocean. Most ocean islands are of volcanic origin.

THE VIOLENT EARTH

The Earth's mantle is a bit like a gigantic sea of toffee. The plates forming the Earth's crust float on this sea, and just as there are currents in the sea, so too there are currents in the molten rock of the mantle. Rising currents may force the plates apart. Molten rock wells up through the crack, creating new crystal rock. Sinking currents may drag the plates together, and cause mountains to form at the buckled edges. Any kind of movement can shake the very foundations of the world we live on. This causes earthquakes, avalanches and landslides, and gigantic waves in the sea called tsunami. It also creates cracks or weak spots through which molten rock breaks to form volcanoes. Our planet is restless and sometimes violent, and every year brings natural disasters.

Volcanoes

Fortunately for most of us, these natural disasters almost always occur along joins between the plates. Elsewhere the crust is mostly strong and stable. However, many people live close to the joins, and there are some places where volcanoes or earthquakes often occur. These include New Zealand and Japan, countries such as Greece and Italy in the Mediterranean Sea, and much of the western edge of America.

Some volcanoes are extinct. They will never erupt again. Some are active and others are dormant, or sleeping. They have not erupted for a long time, but may do so again. Often they are blocked by a plug of very hard rock which seals in the molten rock like a cork seals a bottle.

Famous Eruptions

In ancient Roman times people thought that Vesuvius, a volcano near Naples, was extinct. They built towns around the foot of the volcano, and fine villas on its slopes. Their crops grew well in the fertile volcanic soil. But Vesuvius was not extinct. It was just very well plugged. For 16 years slight earthquakes shook the area, and gradually the plug in Vesuvius was loosened. Then in the year AD 79 the volcano exploded. Hot gases shattered the plug and blasted it into the air, together with a mass of ashes and rock. A thick layer of ashes buried the town of Pompeii. Steam from the eruption mixed with the ashes to make a mixture like liquid concrete. This flowed down and buried Herculaneum, a town on the other side of Vesuvius. Both towns lay hidden and forgotten for 1700 years before being

The new island of Surtsey pouring out a column of gas and smoke.

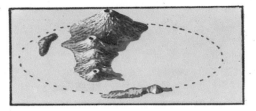
The Krakatoa islands before 1883.

After the 1883 explosion.

Anak Krakatoa (child of Krakatoa) appeared in the 1920s.

found and uncovered by archeologists.

In explosive volcanoes a lot of gas is trapped in the molten rock, which is known as magma. As the magma surges up, bubbles of gas grow suddenly bigger, and burst. Their explosions can hurl the magma high into the air, and break it into millions of fragments.

A violent explosion occurred on the Greek island of Santorini around 1500 BC, making the biggest bang the world has ever known, and destroying most of the island. A similar but less powerful volcanic explosion happened in 1883 when Krakatoa erupted. It had been dormant for 200 years. Then an earthquake tore open the sea bed nearby. A fishing fleet was sucked down to its doom, and the sea water rushed into the fiery depths of Krakatoa. The cold water meeting the molten rock set off a series of mighty explosions, waking people from their sleep 5,000 kilometres away. A cloud of ash rose far into the sky, causing darkness for three days over a vast area. And the fine dusts created strangely brilliant sunsets all around the world.

When the eruption was over, most of Krakatoa had disappeared. In its place was a huge sea-filled crater. Yet even worse than the eruption itself were the towering tsunami waves which spread from Krakatoa. They swept coastal towns and drowned nearly 40,000 people.

Volcanoes can give birth to islands, as well as destroying them. The whole of Iceland is of volcanic origin and off its coast is one of the world's newest islands, Surtsey. It was born in volcanic eruptions in 1963 and has since grown larger. Already seals and sea birds live there.

Sleeping Giants
The volcanoes on the Pacific island of Hawaii are famous quiet volcanoes. Holiday-makers visit the island to look down into the craters where molten rock

bubbles gently, or flows smoothly over the rim. Tourists also visit intermediate volcanoes like Etna, Stromboli and Vulcano near Italy.

Earthquakes

During an earthquake the Earth's crust moves, and the ground shakes —or quakes. There are many minor earthquakes each year which go unnoticed. But sometimes they can be so violent that buildings topple, lives are lost and great cracks open up in the ground.

Earthquakes usually occur where the plates of the Earth's crust grind against each other. This causes tension in the rocks, and when it becomes too great they shift and split. The rock movements cause shock waves which start deep underground. The point on the surface above is called the epicentre, and is the scene of the greatest destruction, but shock waves travel out from the epicentre just as

ripples spread out when you drop a stone in a pond.

Earthquakes are terrible enough anyway, but they often trigger off additional destruction. Quakes can unleash landslides, avalanches, and tsunami. Tsunami travel across oceans as fast as jet airliners, and when they reach shallow coastal waters they can rise to a terrifying 85 metres high.

China is one of the countries worst affected by earthquakes. They have caused terrible loss of life. The worst, in 1556, killed over 800,000 people. On the far right is an early Chinese earthquake detector, or seismograph. An earth tremor opened the dragons' jaws, and the balls dropped into the mouths of the toads below.

Scientists are trying to find ways of forecasting earthquakes, so that people can be warned to leave danger areas in time. Animals may offer a clue. It is claimed that they sometimes behave oddly before quakes, perhaps sensing changes unnoticed by people.

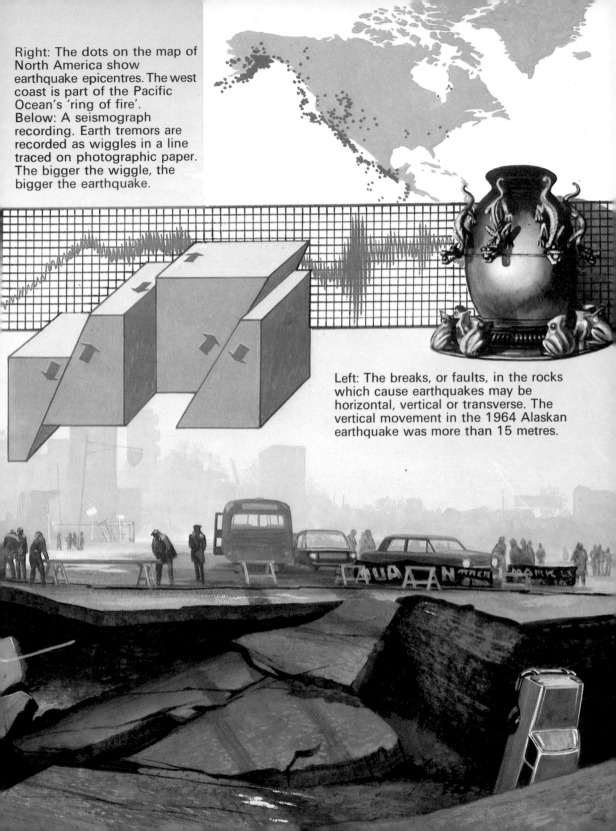

Right: The dots on the map of North America show earthquake epicentres. The west coast is part of the Pacific Ocean's 'ring of fire'.

Below: A seismograph recording. Earth tremors are recorded as wiggles in a line traced on photographic paper. The bigger the wiggle, the bigger the earthquake.

Left: The breaks, or faults, in the rocks which cause earthquakes may be horizontal, vertical or transverse. The vertical movement in the 1964 Alaskan earthquake was more than 15 metres.

THE CLIMATE AND WEATHER

Climate is the general weather of a region. Both climate and weather depend on the atmosphere, the blanket of air that surrounds the Earth. We cannot see the Earth's atmosphere, but it surrounds us all, and stretches tens of kilometres above the ground. It consists mainly of the gases nitrogen and oxygen. The higher above the ground one goes, the thinner is the atmosphere. On top of a high mountain there is hardly enough air to breathe.

Air Pressure
Like everything else, the air has weight, and is kept in place by gravity. Although we are not aware of it, the air presses down on us. This pressure changes with altitude, or height—the higher one rises, the less air there is above, and the lower the pressure. It also changes with the weather. A region of low pressure is called a depression. It usually brings changeable, windy and wet weather. A high pressure area is called an anticyclone. This generally means stable and fine weather.

Air Currents
The atmosphere, like the ocean, is always on the move, and as it swirls and eddies, the weather changes. This movement is caused mainly by the Sun, wind and water. When the Sun rises, it warms the air and the ground. The warm air rises, and its pressure drops. But as it rises it gets cooler. So it sinks again, and its pressure rises. When the Sun sets, the air cools. It sinks, and its pressure rises.

These rising and falling currents of air create wind—which is just moving air. Winds blow from cold, high pressure regions to warm, low pressure ones.

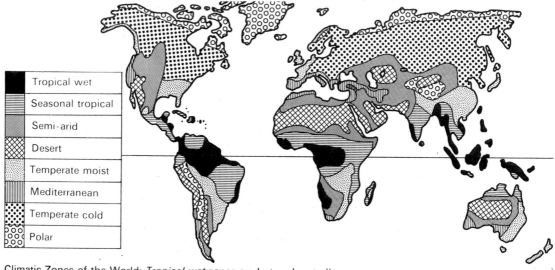

Tropical wet

Seasonal tropical

Semi-arid

Desert

Temperate moist

Mediterranean

Temperate cold

Polar

Climatic Zones of the World: *Tropical wet* zones are hot and wet all year round; *seasonal tropical* zones have a distinct rainy season and are fairly dry the rest of the year; the *semi-arid* and *desert* regions are dry, with little or no rain; *temperate moist* zones have fairly moderate weather all year; *Mediterranean* climates have hot dry summers and rainy winters; *temperate cold* climates have short, hot summers and cold, snowy winters; *polar* regions are cold deserts.

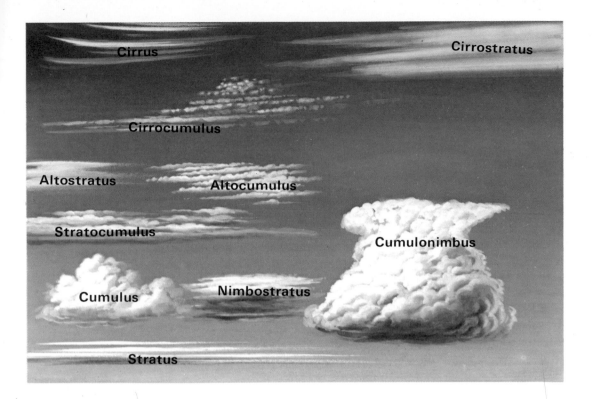

Cirrus · Cirrostratus · Cirrocumulus · Altostratus · Altocumulus · Stratocumulus · Cumulonimbus · Cumulus · Nimbostratus · Stratus

The Water Exchange

In warm weather water evaporates. It is carried up in the air as water vapour. The warmer the air is, the more water vapour it can hold. When warm wet air cools, it can no longer hold all the water. So some of the vapour turns back into droplets of water. This is why dew often forms at night. The air cools after sunset, and some of its water vapour forms droplets of dew. Mist, fog and clouds are all formed like this. So are snow, hail and frost.

Cloud Patterns

Clouds are exactly like mist or fog, but they are held up in the sky by rising currents of air. When the droplets are very thick they join up to create drops of water, which then fall as rain. You can see some of the many kinds of cloud in the picture above. There are two main types,

those with 'cumulus' in their names, and those with 'stratus'.

The cumulus types are 'heap' or cauliflower clouds. They rise up in heaps on a flat base. They form above powerful rising columns of air. The lower ones, like cumulonimbus, often bring showers, but do not usually last very long.

The Rain-Bringers

Stratus clouds form a layer like a thin film across the sky. They may last a long time, bringing long spells of rain or snow.

Stratus clouds also act like a blanket. They trap warm air by stopping it rising further. This explains why cloudy weather is often warm, especially at night and in winter.

In bright weather there is nothing to stop the heat being lost. Bright winter nights are often frosty.

CRUEL WEATHER

Without rain Earth would be a dead planet. But too much causes floods, and too little causes droughts. Both can cause devastation and famine. So can wind, especially when it races along at nearly 500 km/h in a tornado. Tornadoes are also called twisters, because the air twists, or spins. A snaking funnel of cool air sinks down from a cloud. Warm air whirls up the funnel at fantastic speed, sucking up anything in its path, from houses to railway coaches. Objects caught in a tornado's path are totally destroyed because they explode in the partial vacuum at the centre. Buildings just to the side of the tornado's narrow passage are unharmed. Fortunately, tornadoes are rare except in parts of North America.

Hurricanes are tropical storms 'fuelled' by warm, moist air above the sea. They whirl more slowly than tornadoes, but cover a much larger area. Their greatest threat is that they carry torrential rain and drive massive waves before them.

Even 'ordinary' storms can create widespread destruction, especially if they are accompanied by very high tides. Then the sea may be driven thundering over the land. When this happened in the Straits of Dover in 1953, most of south-west Netherlands was submerged and nearly 2,000 people drowned.

A hurricane seen from space. At the centre is the 'eye'—the calm in the centre of the storm. The picture shows how winds spiral around the hurricane's eye.

Lightning is a spark of electricity which flows within a cloud, between clouds, or from a cloud to the ground. It is very hot and can start fires and tear down trees. As the lightning burns its way through the air it creates a shock wave which is the noise we hear as thunder. So lightning and thunder happen at the same moment. We see the lightning first because light travels much faster than sound.

FARMING

In very early times there were no farmers. The first men hunted wild animals, and they gathered wild plants, berries, nuts, fruits, roots and seeds. In a few parts of the world people still live like this. But in most places mankind has depended on farming to supply food for thousands of years. Today more people work on farms than at any other job.

Subsistence Farming

In some countries, particularly in Africa and Asia, almost everyone is a farmer. Often there is no other work. In regions where the land is not very fertile, or where there are few tools and machines to help, each family or group produces just enough food for itself. This is called subsistence farming. Many subsistence farmers have to move from place to place every few years. They clear a patch of land and farm it. After several growing seasons the soil loses its goodness, and becomes infertile. So the people must move on and find a fresh patch.

The World's Farms

Over the world as a whole more than half the people are farmers, but they are not equally shared among countries. In Britain only two people out of every hundred are farmers. In North America the proportion is six in every hundred, in Australia nine, and in Germany seven. These countries and many others like them are modern industrial nations. Most of their citizens work in offices and factories. In these countries farms are run like factories. Farmers have modern machines to help do the work more efficiently and quickly. They use more fertilizers to help the crops grow well, and they have all sorts of chemicals to prevent disease and kill harmful insects.

Farmers in many parts of Africa and India work with simple tools, exactly like the ones their ancestors used hundreds or perhaps thousands of years ago. And they grow 'old fashioned' crops and breed the same kinds of animals.

The two main types of farming are arable farming, or crop growing, and livestock farming. Around one tenth of the land in the world is used for crop growing, while grazing or pasture land for livestock covers roughly twice that area. So three tenths, or a little over a quarter, of the Earth is farmland.

Arable Farming

Where the land is good enough, farmers usually grow crops rather than raise animals. This is partly because animals

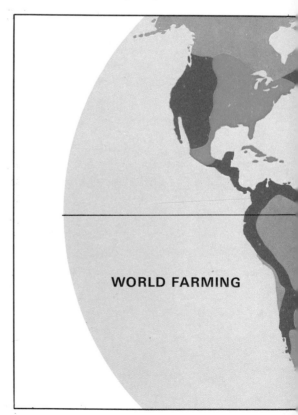

WORLD FARMING

can graze on land which is too poor for arable farming, and partly because arable farms provide greater food value than livestock raising. The crops growing on a patch of land can feed about five times as many people as the meat from animals grazing on the same sized patch.

The most important arable crops are cereals. These include wheat, rye, barley, maize, oats, millet and rice. Millions of people around the world live mainly on bread, which is usually made from wheat or rye, while in eastern countries such as China and India rice is the main food. The other main groups of arable crops are fruit and vegetables.

In addition there are arable crops like tea, coffee and cocoa from which drinks are made, and others such as cotton, flax, hemp and rubber, which provide us with much of our clothing and other useful materials.

Livestock Farming
Livestock farming gives us meat and eggs, as well as milk and milk products such as butter and cheese. But it also provides materials like leather and wool. In some parts of the world it provides a vital form of transport and power in the form of draught animals.

The most important animals raised on livestock farms around the world are cattle, sheep and pigs, and various kinds of poultry like chickens and ducks.

Many farms combine arable and livestock farming. This is called mixed farming, and is especially common in northern Europe, America, Australia and New Zealand.

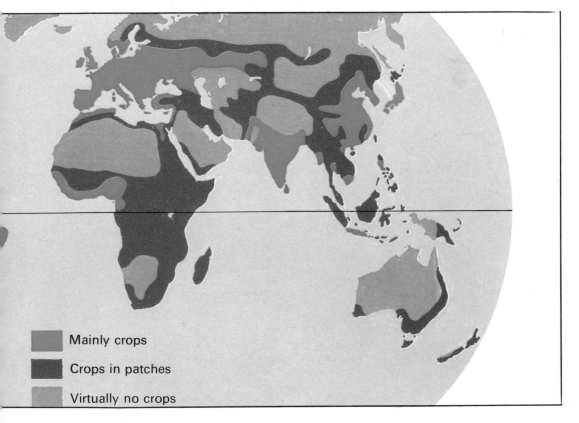

■ Mainly crops

■ Crops in patches

■ Virtually no crops

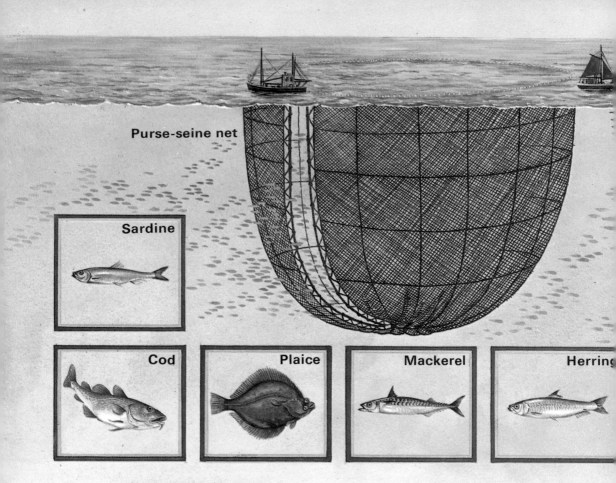

Purse-seine net

Sardine

Cod

Plaice

Mackerel

Herring

FISHING

Fishing is a major source of food. The main fishing grounds lie on the continental shelves around the continents. The illustration shows the main fishing methods. The purse-seine net hangs from buoys, and catches shoals of fish near the surface. Once the fish are inside, the net is drawn shut like a purse. The drift net also catches fish in surface waters. In trawling, the bag-shaped net is towed along near the sea bed. The long-line carries hundreds of hooked lines.

Modern fishing boats carry electronic equipment to locate shoals of fish. In the past 50 years, fishing methods have become so efficient that many fish are becoming scarce. Most of the popular fish for eating are shown above. The herring is already in short supply, and others soon may be. One answer to this problem is for us to learn to eat other kinds of fish. Fish farming provides a second answer. Fish could be raised in giant underwater pens. Dolphins might be used as 'sheepdogs', while the 'shepherds' could work in mini-submarines.

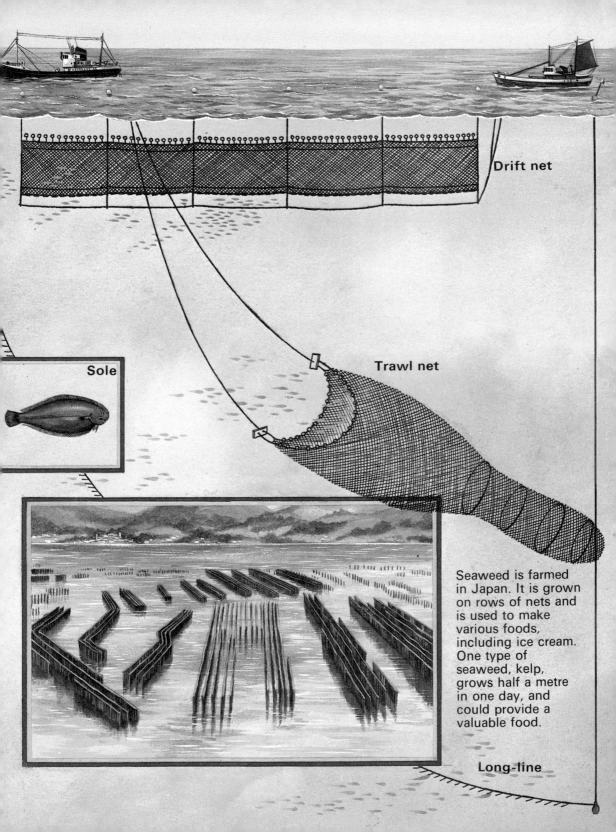

Drift net

Trawl net

Sole

Seaweed is farmed in Japan. It is grown on rows of nets and is used to make various foods, including ice cream. One type of seaweed, kelp, grows half a metre in one day, and could provide a valuable food.

Long-line

EARTH'S RESOURCES

Our world is becoming ever more crowded, and filled with machines and gadgets. Making these things requires vast amounts of raw materials. We also need vast amounts of energy to drive machines, to provide heat and light, and to power all forms of transport.

Some of the raw materials needed for manufacturing and energy are grown. Trees provide wood for fuel, furniture, building, paper and so on. Plants and animals provide materials such as wool, cotton and leather. But today most of the raw materials and fuels we use come from the ground.

Minerals

Vital metals such as iron, copper, tin, silver and gold are all minerals. They come from the rocks of the Earth's crust. Sometimes they are found near the

surface, but often deep mines must be dug to reach them. The metals are always mixed with unwanted materials in a substance called ore. The ore has to be treated to extract the pure metal.

Many minerals other than metals are also mined, quarried or dug out of the ground. They include the rocks themselves, for buildings; sand, for concrete and for making glass; fertilizers; and even the talc in talcum powder.

Fuels

Most fuel for energy and power also comes from deep underground, in the form of oil, gas and coal. These 'fossil'

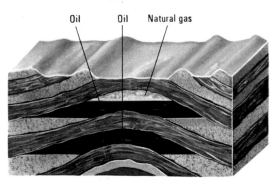

Much of the Earth's crust is made up of layers of different kinds of rock. Some layers consist of waterproof or impermeable rock (shown brown in the diagram). In others the rock is porous, or full of holes rather like a sponge (blue in the diagram). In places the great pressures in the crust bend or fold the layers of rock, as in the diagram. When this happens, any oil or gas in the porous rock collects in the folds, and is trapped there, sealed in by the impermeable rock above.

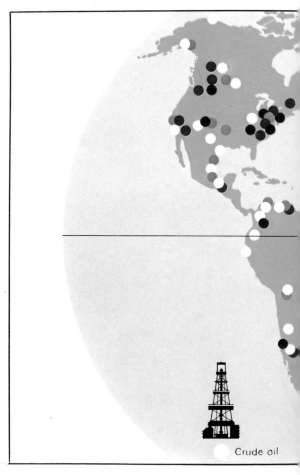

Crude oil

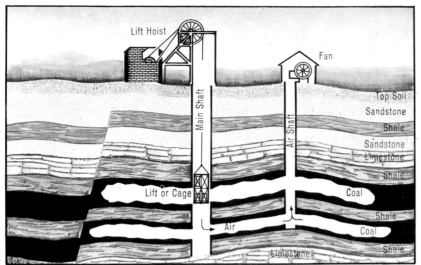

Coal is often found in layers or seams. Shafts are dug down through the upper layers of rock until coal is reached. Miners then tunnel sideways from the shafts, digging out the coal, which is hoisted to the surface by the lift. The fan keeps fresh air moving through the mine.

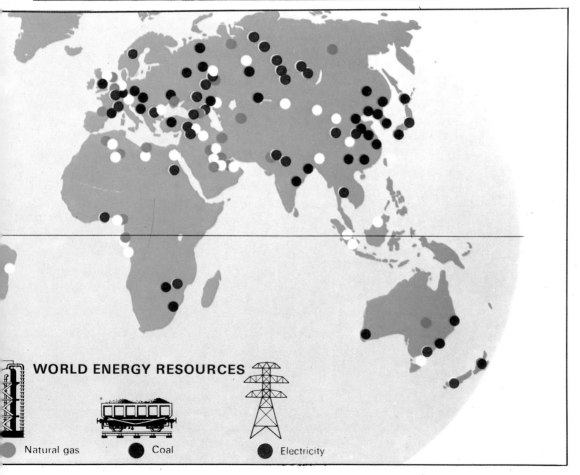

WORLD ENERGY RESOURCES

Natural gas   Coal   Electricity

fuels were created millions of years ago from the remains of plants and animals. These remains became deeply buried, and the great pressure far underground helped turn forest trees into coal, and the remains of countless tiny plants and animals into oil and gas.

Coal

Some coal is near the surface and can be reached by open cast mining. The soil and other surface layers are simply dug away to reveal the coal, but usually it is mined from deep below the ground. However, extracting coal remains an expensive task, and for some time the world has been using more oil and gas and less coal. These fuels are easier and cheaper to obtain and to transport, and they give out more heat.

Finding Oil and Gas

The first step is to find a likely spot. Geologists study the structure of the rocks using scientific instruments such as seismographs (earthquake detectors). They fire explosive charges in holes in the ground, and measure the tiny quakes or shock waves that bounce back off the various layers of rock below. When a promising spot is located, the next step is to drill a hole or well. This may have to go hundreds or even thousands of metres down into the rock. When the oil or gas is reached, it is usually under such great pressure that it shoots up to the surface by itself. But sometimes it must be pumped up. In either case, once it is flowing it is controlled by taps and valves, and transported along pipelines.

The raw or crude oil must be treated at a refinery before it can be used. There it is purified, and broken down into many different fuels and other materials, ready for transport around the world by pipelines, road vehicles and giant oil tankers.

Coal and oil are burnt as fuels, but they also provide the raw materials for all sorts of other materials including many plastics and 'man made materials' for clothing. All three fossil fuels—coal, oil and gas—may be used directly as fuels, or they can be burned to generate electricity.

All these minerals and fossil fuels form part of the Earth's resources, and they are all limited. There is a certain amount of them in the world, and no more. Eventually they will run out. We must conserve what we have, and we must look for new fuels and new sources or raw materials.

One of the first steps has been to start harvesting the resources of the seas and oceans. Over a third of the world's oil is now produced from oil rigs—giant structures out at sea from which oil wells are drilled in the sea bed. Already some minerals, like salt and magnesium, are extracted from the sea. But at the moment, the most serious problem is fuel. Some experts believe that we may run out of oil and gas in 50 or a hundred years, and we may run out of coal a couple of hundred years later.

Hydro-electricity

The map on page 53 shows the main areas around the world where the three fossil fuels are mined. It also shows where hydro-electricity is an important source of energy. This is produced by fast flowing rivers and waterfalls. The water spins turbines which generate electricity. Hydro-electric power is especially valuable in mountainous countries like Norway, Switzerland and Scotland, and in countries with little coal.

Nuclear Energy

Nuclear or atomic power is another way of generating electricity without using up fossil fuels. It produces an enormous amount of energy from a minute amount of the mineral uranium. One kilogramme of uranium burnt in a nuclear reactor generates as much energy as $4\frac{1}{2}$ million kilogrammes of coal.

Geothermal Energy

Some other possible sources of energy for the future are described on page 208. There is one other natural resource. Geothermal energy (see illustration) taps the same underground heat that sets volcanoes erupting and geysers and hot springs bubbling. In some areas of the world water lies deep underground above hot volcanic rock. Engineers can drill down to this water and use its steam to drive turbines for generating electric power. Where a hot spring bubbles up to the surface, its water can simply be piped around homes, offices, and factories to provide natural central heating.

Scientists are also studying the possibility of using this underground heat in regions where there is no water trapped above the hot rock. They hope to drill deep holes down into the hot rock. Water flowing down one hole would turn to steam and rise up another hole.

Geothermal energy, hydro-electric power and other forms of natural energy from the Sun, the wind and the sea, will last as long as our planet. Building the necessary structures and equipment costs a lot, but the energy is clean and safe, and it wastes none of our planet's valuable and diminishing resources.

HIGHEST MOUNTAINS

	metres
Everest (Himalaya – Nepal/Tibel)	8,848
Godwin Austen (Karakoram – India)	8,611
Kanchenjunga (Himalaya – Nepal)	8,579
Makalu (Himalaya – Nepal/Tibet)	8,470
Dhaulagiri (Himalaya – Nepal)	8,172
Nanga Parbat (Himalaya – India)	8,126
Annapurna (Himalaya – Nepal)	8,075
Gasherbrum (Karakoram – India)	8,068
Gosainthan (Himalaya – Tibet)	8,013
Nanda Devi (Himalaya – India)	7,817
Aconcagua (Andes – Argentina)	6,960
McKinley (Alaska – USA)	6,194
Kilimanjaro (Tanzania)	5,888
Elborus (Caucasus – USSR)	5,633
Mont Blanc (Alps – France)	4,810

LONGEST RIVERS

	km
Nile (Africa)	6,679
Amazon (South America)	6,276
Mississippi-Missouri-Red Rock (North America)	6,231
Ob-Irtysh (USSR)	5,150
Yangtze (China)	5,150
Zaire (Africa)	4,828
Lena (USSR)	4,828
Amur (Asia)	4,506
Yenisei (USSR)	4,506
Hwang Ho (China)	4,345
Niger (Africa)	4,184
Mekong (South East Asia)	4,184

LARGEST ISLANDS

	sq km
Greenland (North Atlantic)	2,130,265
New Guinea (South West Pacific)	794,090
Borneo (South West Pacific)	751,078
Madagascar (Indian Ocean)	589,683
Baffin Island (Canadian Arctic)	476,066
Sumatra (Indian Ocean)	431,982
Great Britain (North Atlantic)	229,522
Honshu (North West Pacific)	226,087
Ellesmere (Canadian Arctic)	198,393
Victoria Island (Canadian Arctic)	192,695

THE CONTINENTS

	km^2
Asia	42,700,000
Africa	29,860,000
North America	24,307,000
South America	18,221,000
Antarctica	15,500,000
Europe	9,800,000
Australia	7,635,000

THE OCEANS

	km^2
Pacific	181,000,000
Atlantic	106,000,000
Indian	73,490,000
Arctic	14,350,000

World of Nature

THE STORY OF LIVING THINGS

Traces of simple plants in ancient rocks suggest that life existed on the Earth as long as 3,000 million years ago. We do not know when animals first appeared, but they were certainly around by 1,000 million years ago. By 600 million years ago, shellfish and other small animals were very common in the seas. Their remains—known as fossils—occur in rocks of this age in many parts of the world. As far as we know, all life was still found in the water at this time, but simple

plants began to live on land soon after that, and they were followed by small animals without backbones.

The First Land Animals

The earliest backboned animals were the fishes. Most remained in the water like today's fishes, but it seems likely that about 300 million years ago some young fishes began to crawl about at the edges of the numerous swamps, feeding on worms and insects. These fishes gradually evolved, or changed, into the first amphibians—the ancestors of our frogs and toads—although they had tails and remained rather fish-like. They had to return to the water to breed. During the next few million years, their bodies improved and became better adapted for life on land. The amphibians had evolved into the first reptiles—the forerunners of the great dinosaurs and of today's snakes and lizards. For about 100 million years, the reptiles truly ruled the world. Huge

Father of the Dinosaurs

The first reptiles were small, sharp-toothed animals with rather short, sprawling legs. They probably dragged their bodies through the swampy forests and ate insects and small amphibians. The earliest did not look much different from amphibians. Later, their legs became longer and stronger and the animals were able to lift their bodies off the ground. This enabled them to move more quickly. The hind legs of some reptiles became larger than the front legs. One such reptile was *Euparkeria*, seen below, which lived about 210 million years ago. When in a hurry it ran almost upright on its hind legs. A long tail helped to keep its balance as it chased flying insects. All of the dinosaurs and today's birds and crocodiles may well have descended from an animal like *Euparkeria*.

Many dinosaurs were huge creatures. *Apatosaurus* was nearly 25 m long, and many others would have towered over a man, as shown here. But some dinosaurs were small: the insect-eating *Compsognathus*, for example, was not much bigger than a chicken.

Parasaurolophus

Tyrannosaurus

plant-eating and flesh-eating dinosaurs wandered over the land, while other reptiles lived in the sea and even flew in the air.

Plant Life
The first land plants must have been very small and not unlike some of today's seaweeds and mosses, but by 300 million years ago they had evolved into giants topping 30 metres in height. These giants were quite unlike today's trees and were

Apatosaurus

Man

Ornithomimus

Stegosaurus

Compsognathus

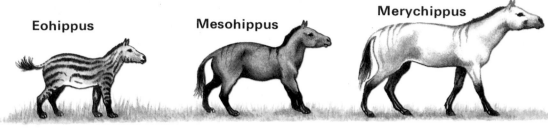

Eohippus

Mesohippus

Merychippus

more closely related to modern ferns and horsetails. They grew in extensive swamps and their remains now form our coal supplies. Cone-bearing trees similar to today's pines and firs became common about 280 million years ago. Along with the ferns and their relatives, they dominated the Earth until not much more than 100 million years ago, when flowering plants began to take over.

The First Birds

The birds were evolving from reptiles while all these changes were going on in the plant world. It is thought that the first birds evolved from some small types of tree-climbing dinosaur, whose scales gradually became converted into feathers. The earliest known bird is called *Archaeopteryx* and its remains have been found in rocks about 150 million years old.

The Rise of the Mammals

About 100 million years ago, the dinosaur population fell drastically and by about 80 million years ago none of these great beasts remained alive. They were rapidly replaced by warm-blooded mammals—the group of animals to which we ourselves belong. Mammals had been in existence for many millions of years but they had always been small and there were probably not many of them.

Early mammals had probably been insect-eaters, but now they were free to exploit plants and other animals. Many of them became grazing creatures, while others became powerful flesh-eaters—the ancestors of our cats and dogs. Some, like the reptiles before them, reverted to life in the water. By about 100,000 years ago nearly all of today's mammals had appeared, including people.

Many of the early mammals' bones were preserved, or fossilized, in the rock. We can see from these fossils how the animals evolved into modern types. One of the best known histories is that of the horse. Some of the stages in its evolution are shown on this page.

Pliohippus

Modern horse

Bush-antlered
deer

Scimitar cat

REBUILDING A DINOSAUR

No person has ever seen a living dinosaur. The dinosaurs died out many millions of years before the first human beings appeared on the Earth. We know about these ancient reptiles, however, because they left fossils in the rocks.

When animals die their bodies normally rot, but sometimes their bones are preserved as fossils. One way in which an animal can be fossilized is shown at the top of these pages. Suppose a prehistoric creature such as *Iguanodon* died by falling from a cliff into the sea. Its skin and soft flesh would soon rot, but its skeleton would sink to the bottom and it would be covered by sand or mud.

Slowly, over millions of years, this sand or mud would harden into solid rock. The bones, locked inside the rock, would also harden and would themselves turn to stone. Millions of years later the rocks may be lifted up to form dry land, and the fossilized bones may become exposed.

A Bone Puzzle

People who collect and study fossils are called **palaeontologists**. The palaeontologist in the picture below has found the skeleton of *Iguanodon* in some rocks. She is very careful as she chips and brushes the loose rock from around the bones. A great deal of work, usually by a whole team of people, is necessary before all of the bones can be uncovered and removed from the rock. More painstaking work will enable the palaeontologists to

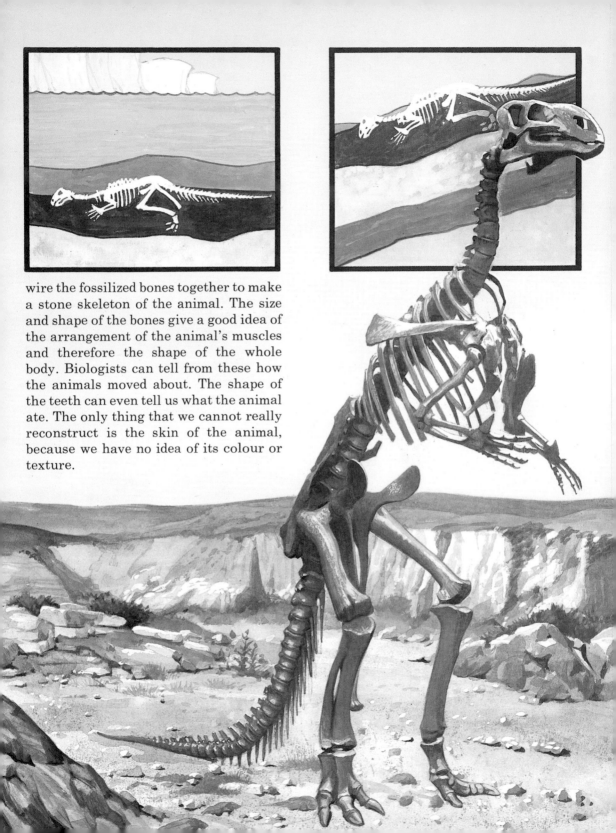

wire the fossilized bones together to make a stone skeleton of the animal. The size and shape of the bones give a good idea of the arrangement of the animal's muscles and therefore the shape of the whole body. Biologists can tell from these how the animals moved about. The shape of the teeth can even tell us what the animal ate. The only thing that we cannot really reconstruct is the skin of the animal, because we have no idea of its colour or texture.

THE WORLD OF PLANTS

The living world is divided into two great groups—the Plant World and the Animal World. The main difference between the two groups lies in their feeding methods. Animals have to take in ready-made food in the form of plants or other animals, but most plants can actually make their own food from simple substances in the air and water. This process is called photosynthesis (see the box on page 68). The plants need sunlight for making food, and they also need the green pigment or colouring matter called chlorophyll. This is why most plants are green.

Plants without Flowers

Almost all the flowers that surround us in our gardens and in the countryside bear flowers at certain times of the year. But it is not true that all plants have flowers. Many do not even have stems and leaves.

The simplest plants are called **bacteria.** These are microscopic living things, found almost everywhere—even our bodies are full of them. Some bacteria cause disease and are called germs, but the great majority are harmless. They obtain food and energy by chemical methods—sometimes breaking down plant or animal matter and sometimes building up food from carbon dioxide gas. The bacteria reproduce themselves simply by splitting into two pieces.

The fungi are the moulds and toadstools—a very large group of organisms without chlorophyll. They take their food from other plants and animals, both living and dead. Their bodies consist of masses of hair-like threads, which cluster tightly together to form the familiar toadstools. Some biologists do not think

that the fungi are plants at all, but they are very much like the algae in their methods of reproduction. They scatter millions of minute, dust-like spores which grow into new individuals.

The **algae** are simple plants that nearly all live in water. The best known are the seaweeds, but there are many smaller ones that swim freely in the water. Some minute algae live on tree trunks and clothe them with a green film. All the algae contain chlorophyll and make their own food, although many have other pigments that make them brown or red. The plants have no real roots, stems, or leaves. They reproduce by releasing minute spores, which often float freely in the water or air.

Mosses live mainly in damp places, where they form mats or cushions. They have slender stems and small leaves, but only very simple, hair-like roots. They all make their own food, and they reproduce by scattering spores. These are formed in capsules which grow up from the plants.

Liverworts are close relatives of the mosses. Some have moss-like stems and leaves, but others look more like flat seaweeds that are growing on damp rocks and soil.

The **ferns** also reproduce by scattering spores, but the plants are generally much larger than mosses, with large leaves and stout stems. These stems are usually under the ground. The spores are carried on the underside of the leaves. Most ferns live in damp places.

Club mosses and **horsetails** are related to the ferns, but they carry their spores in cones at the tips of the stems.

Plants with Seeds

The plants described so far all reproduce by scattering minute spores. These are much simpler than seeds. A seed consists

The Plant Kingdom

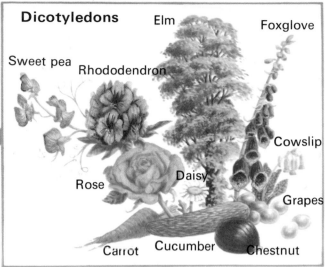

Dicotyledons

Elm

Foxglove

Sweet pea

Rhododendron

Cowslip

Rose

Daisy

Grapes

Carrot

Cucumber

Chestnut

Dicotyledons are the group of flowering plants in which the leaves are rather broad and net-veined. The seeds contain two tiny leaves.

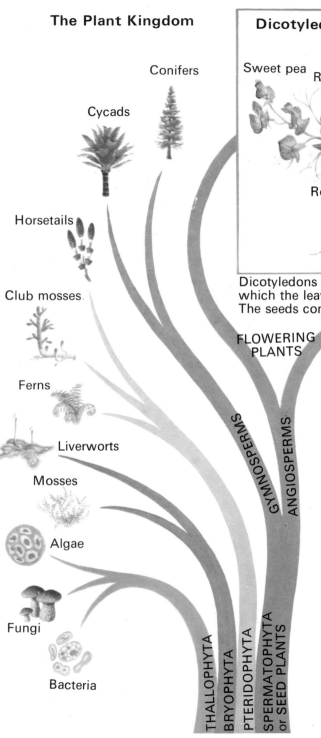

Conifers

Cycads

Horsetails

Club mosses

Ferns

Liverworts

Mosses

Algae

Fungi

Bacteria

FLOWERING PLANTS

Monocotyledons are the group of flowering plants in which the leaves are generally strap-shaped. The seeds contain just one tiny leaf.

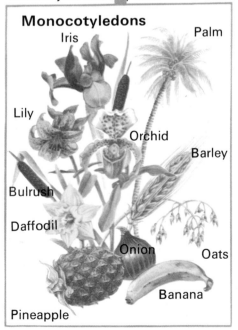

Monocotyledons

Iris

Palm

Lily

Orchid

Barley

Bulrush

Daffodil

Onion

Oats

Banana

Pineapple

GYMNOSPERMS

ANGIOSPERMS

THALLOPHYTA

BRYOPHYTA

PTERIDOPHYTA

SPERMATOPHYTA or SEED PLANTS

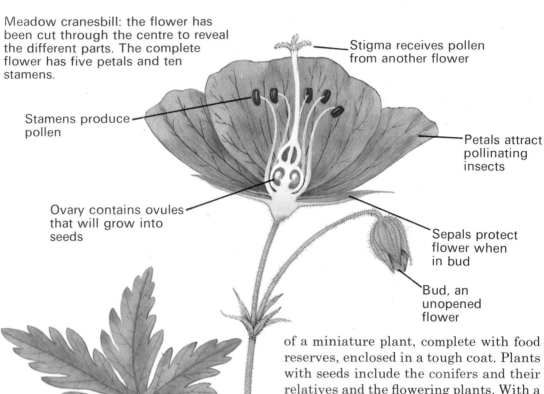

Meadow cranesbill: the flower has been cut through the centre to reveal the different parts. The complete flower has five petals and ten stamens.

Stigma receives pollen from another flower

Stamens produce pollen

Petals attract pollinating insects

Ovary contains ovules that will grow into seeds

Sepals protect flower when in bud

Bud, an unopened flower

Photosynthesis
Photosynthesis, the plant's food-making process, takes place mainly in the leaves. These are arranged so that they get as much sunlight as possible, for light is essential to the process. The green chlorophyll traps the light energy, which the plant then uses to combine water and carbon dioxide gas. Sugar is formed for food and oxygen is given off.

of a miniature plant, complete with food reserves, enclosed in a tough coat. Plants with seeds include the conifers and their relatives and the flowering plants. With a few exceptions, they all have roots to hold them firmly in the ground and to absorb water, and they have stems and leaves. Both stems and leaves are extremely varied in shape and size.

The **conifers** include the pines, firs, spruces, and other trees that carry their seeds in woody cones hanging from or sitting on their branches. The cones first appear as little red buds, but they do not develop further until they have been pollinated with pollen from the yellowish male cones. The pollen is carried by the wind, and when it gets into the little red cones it triggers off the growth of the seeds. The cones open when they are ripe and the winged seeds blow away. **Cycads** are large-leaved plants that look rather like palm trees, but they are related to the conifers and carry their seeds in huge cones at the tops of their trunks.

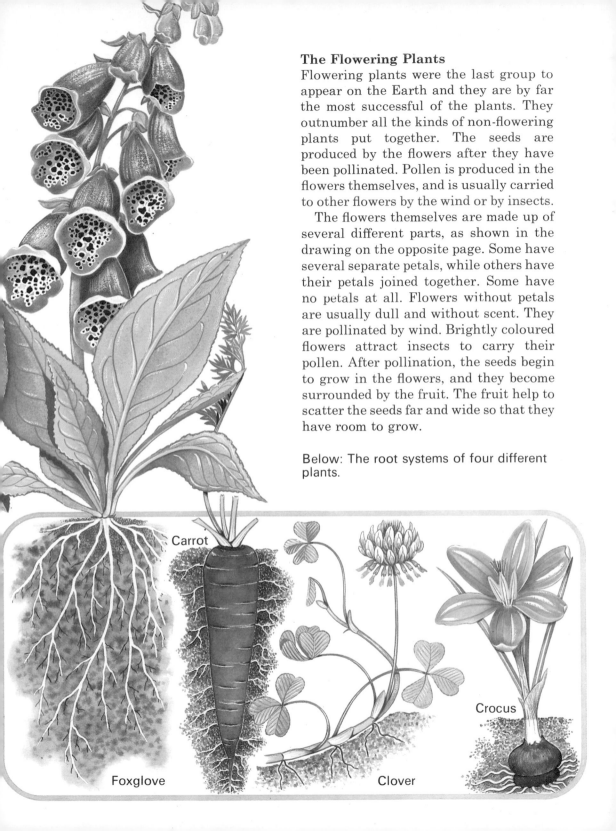

The Flowering Plants

Flowering plants were the last group to appear on the Earth and they are by far the most successful of the plants. They outnumber all the kinds of non-flowering plants put together. The seeds are produced by the flowers after they have been pollinated. Pollen is produced in the flowers themselves, and is usually carried to other flowers by the wind or by insects.

The flowers themselves are made up of several different parts, as shown in the drawing on the opposite page. Some have several separate petals, while others have their petals joined together. Some have no petals at all. Flowers without petals are usually dull and without scent. They are pollinated by wind. Brightly coloured flowers attract insects to carry their pollen. After pollination, the seeds begin to grow in the flowers, and they become surrounded by the fruit. The fruit help to scatter the seeds far and wide so that they have room to grow.

Below: The root systems of four different plants.

Carrot

Crocus

Foxglove

Clover

Woodland Flowers 1. Early purple orchid 2. Yellow archangel 3. White helleborine 4. Wood anemone 5. Wild strawberry 6. Dog's mercury 7. Bluebell 8. Primrose 9. Wood spurge 10. Early dog violet 11. Wood forget-me-not

Hedgerow and Wayside Flowers 1. White bryony 2. Hedge bindweed
3. Blackberry 4. Honeysuckle 5. Chicory 6. White deadnettle 7. Tufted vetch
8. Teasel 9. Hogweed 10. Cotton thistle

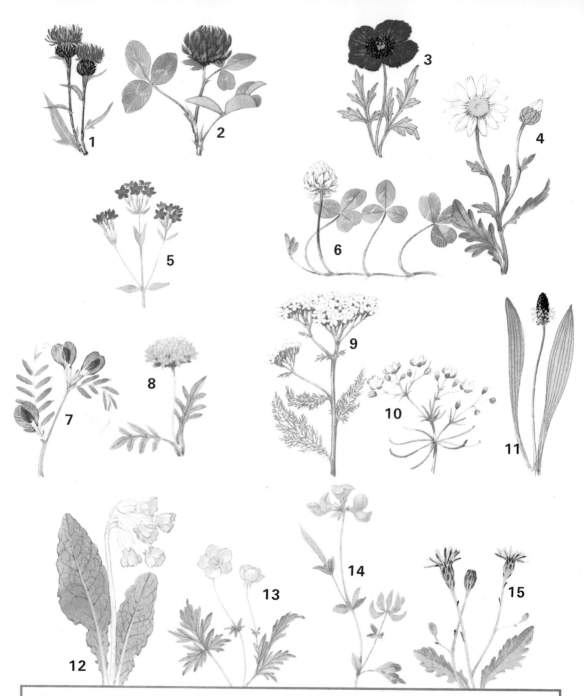

Grassland Flowers 1. Common knapweed 2. Red clover 3. Common poppy 4. Ox-eye daisy 5. Centaury 6. White clover 7. Common vetch 8. Field scabious 9. Yarrow 10. Ragwort 11. Ribwort plantain 12. Cowslip 13. Bulbous buttercup 14. Bird's foot trefoil 15. Common catsear

Flowers of Heath and Moor 1. Bilberry 2. Cowberry 3. Cranberry 4. Ling
5. Bird's eye primrose 6. Alpine willowherb 7. Alpine fleabane 8. Alpine lady's
mantle 9. Bog asphodel 10. Butterwort 11. Spring gentian 12. Grass of Parnassus
13. Broom 14. Gorse

Waterside Flowers 1. Bulrush 2. Great willowherb 3. Flowering rush. 4. Yellow iris 5. Branched bur-reed 6. Marsh pennywort 7. Marsh valerian 8. Common comfrey 9. Purple loosestrife 10. Water mint 11. Marsh orchid 12. Marestail 13. Water crowfoot 14. Water soldier 15. Canadian pondweed

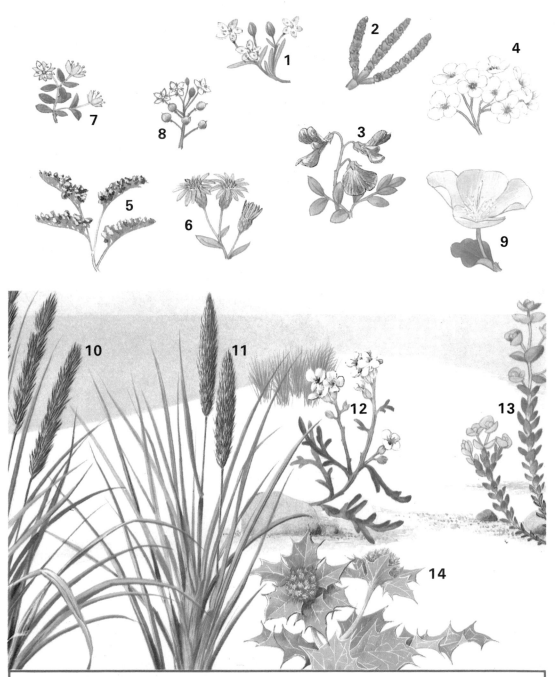

Seaside Flowers 1. Sea spurrey 2. Glasswort 3. Sea pea 4. Sea kale 5. Sea lavender 6. Sea aster 7. Sea purslane 8. Scurvygrass 9. Yellow horned poppy 10. Lyme grass 11. Marram grass 12. Sea rocket 13. Sea spurge 14. Sea holly

Some Common Weeds and Town Flowers 1. Rosebay willowherb 2. Wallflower
3. Oxford ragwort 4. Ivy-leaved toadflax 5. White stonecrop 6. White campion
7. Greater celandine 8. Dandelion

TREES

Trees are plants in which there is just one main woody stem, known as the trunk. This distinguishes them from shrubs and bushes, in which there are several woody stems springing from or near ground level. Mature trees are generally several metres high, and many species become extremely large. In fact, trees are not only the largest plants; they include the largest of all living things. The great redwood trees of California reach heights of over 100 metres, and the wellingtonias, although not so tall, are so massive that they are believed to reach weights approaching 2,000 tonnes.

Despite their size, the trees function in exactly the same way as other plants. They have roots to anchor them in the ground and to absorb water and minerals, and they have green leaves in which they make food by photosynthesis. Because there are so many leaves, the tree needs its strong, woody trunk to hold them all up to the light and to carry all the required water to them. Trees live for many years, and their trunks get thicker each year as new water-carrying tubes are added. These tubes form the annual rings, which can often be seen when a tree is cut down.

Flowering Trees

Most trees are flowering plants. Their flowers may be large and conspicuous, as in the apple, the lilac, and the horse chestnut, but they are often quite small and easily overlooked. Oaks, elms, and ash are among the trees with inconspicuous flowers. Their pollen is scattered by the wind. The flowers generally appear early in the year, before large leaves can get in the way of drifting pollen.

Spruce cones, like all other seed-bearing cones, start life as small red buds (top). Pollen reaches them from the yellowish male cones, and they start to swell. Seeds grow inside them as they turn green and then brown. The ripe brown cones break up to release the winged seeds, but many are eaten by birds.

Non-flowering Trees

The non-flowering trees are the conifers and their relatives. Most of them carry their seeds in woody cones. Their leaves are usually tough and needle-like.

Most conifers are evergreen, meaning that they bear leaves throughout the year. The tough leaves are not harmed by the cold winter winds. Most conifers live in northern lands or on the mountains, but some grow in areas with hot, dry summers. Their tough leaves do not wither in the heat. (The flowering trees are often called broad-leaved trees because their leaves are generally much broader than those of the conifers.) In tropical regions, where growth goes on throughout the year, the trees are evergreen and have rather tough leaves. There are some tough-leaved evergreens in temperate regions such as the British Isles—the holly is a good example—but the flowering trees of such regions generally have more delicate leaves. These leaves fall in the autumn, often turning brilliant red and gold colours before dropping. Trees which lose their leaves for the winter are called deciduous.

Recognizing Trees

Many trees develop characteristic shapes as they grow, as a result of specific patterns of branching. Coniferous trees, for example, tend to be rather conical, especially when young. This is because the main trunk goes on growing and producing whorls of side branches. Flowering trees usually fork and fan out, producing a more rounded outline. In a wood, the trees are crowded and the branches cannot spread out properly. Bark, buds, flowers, and fruits can all be used to identify the trees, but the leaves are the most useful things to look for.

Ash

Plane

Buds The winter buds contain the next season's leaves and sometimes flowers as well.

Branches contain many tiny tubes which carry water and minerals to the leaves and food away from them.

Cherry   Pine

Bark The dead and cracked outer bark protects the living tissues beneath it.

Roots anchor the tree. Hairs on the finest branches absorb water and minerals in the soil.

Rowan

Sycamore

Sweet chestnut

Silver fir

Leaves are where the tree makes its food. Deciduous leaves fall in the autumn, but evergreen leaves remain throughout the year. Cone-bearing trees, such as the silver fir, usually have needle-like leaves but flowering trees generally have broad leaves.

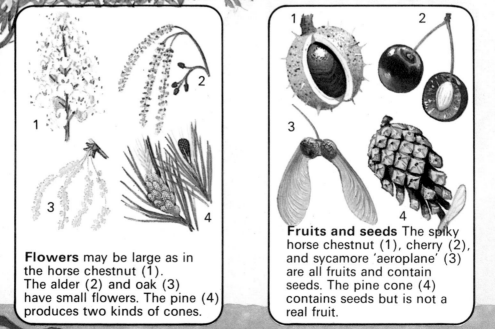

Flowers may be large as in the horse chestnut (1). The alder (2) and oak (3) have small flowers. The pine (4) produces two kinds of cones.

Fruits and seeds The spiky horse chestnut (1), cherry (2), and sycamore 'aeroplane' (3) are all fruits and contain seeds. The pine cone (4) contains seeds but is not a real fruit.

Above: Wych elm showing characteristic winter and summer outlines.
Below and right: Oak fruits (acorns).

Flowering Trees

The seeds of flowering trees are enclosed in fruits and they may have two or three protective coverings. The crinkly walnut seed is enclosed in a woody 'stone', which itself is surrounded by a leathery case when on the tree. The horse chestnut seed, or conker, is enclosed in a spiky capsule. The fruits of the oak, the sweet chestnut, and the beech are thin-walled nuts, with seeds inside them. The nuts themselves sit in a protective cup, or cupule. The sweet chestnut and beech nut are completely surrounded by their cups until they are ripe.

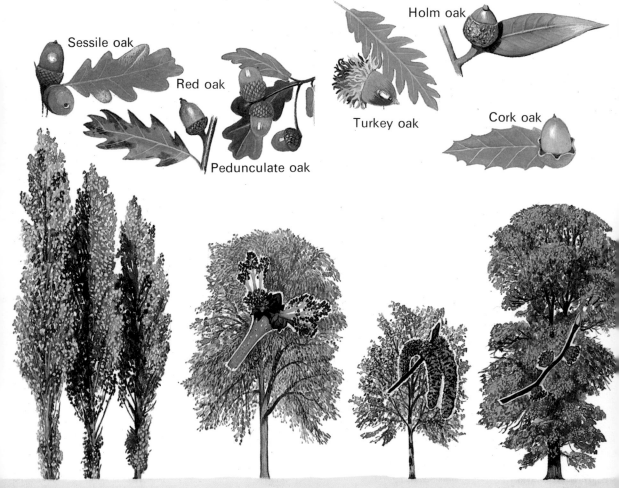

Sessile oak

Red oak

Pedunculate oak

Holm oak

Turkey oak

Cork oak

Lombardy poplar   Ash   Aspen   English elm

Walnut

Horse chestnut

Sweet chestnut

Beech

Common lime

Hornbeam

Crack willow

Silver birch

81

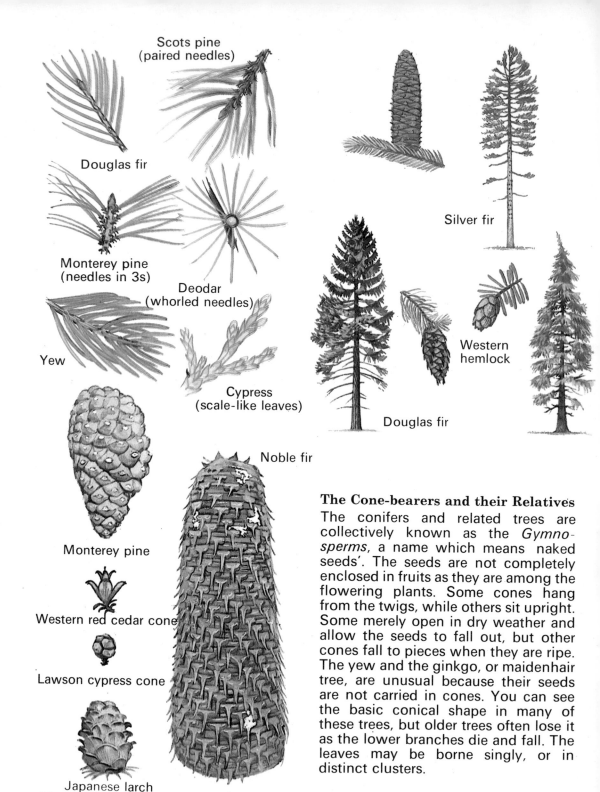

Scots pine
(paired needles)

Douglas fir

Monterey pine
(needles in 3s)

Deodar
(whorled needles)

Yew

Cypress
(scale-like leaves)

Silver fir

Western
hemlock

Douglas fir

Noble fir

Monterey pine

Western red cedar cone

Lawson cypress cone

Japanese larch

The Cone-bearers and their Relatives

The conifers and related trees are collectively known as the *Gymnosperms*, a name which means naked seeds'. The seeds are not completely enclosed in fruits as they are among the flowering plants. Some cones hang from the twigs, while others sit upright. Some merely open in dry weather and allow the seeds to fall out, but other cones fall to pieces when they are ripe. The yew and the ginkgo, or maidenhair tree, are unusual because their seeds are not carried in cones. You can see the basic conical shape in many of these trees, but older trees often lose it as the lower branches die and fall. The leaves may be borne singly, or in distinct clusters.

Grand fir

Scots pine

Corsican pine

Yew

Stone pine
(umbrella pine)

Aleppo pine

Maidenhair tree, showing the
unusual leaf and 'fruit'

Monkey puzzle tree,
or Chile pine

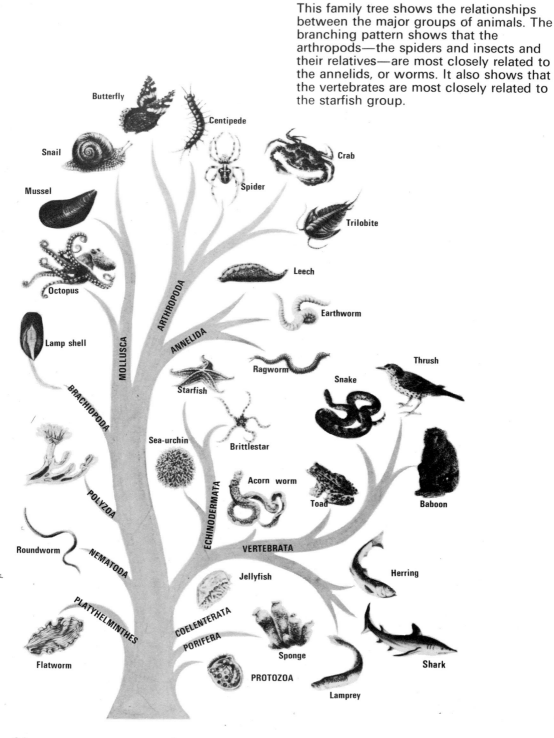

This family tree shows the relationships between the major groups of animals. The branching pattern shows that the arthropods—the spiders and insects and their relatives—are most closely related to the annelids, or worms. It also shows that the vertebrates are most closely related to the starfish group.

Butterfly

Centipede

Snail

Spider

Crab

Mussel

Trilobite

Octopus

ARTHROPODA

Leech

Earthworm

Lamp shell

MOLLUSCA

ANNELIDA

Ragworm

Thrush

Snake

Starfish

BRACHIOPODA

Sea-urchin

Brittlestar

Acorn worm

POLYZOA

ECHINODERMATA

Toad

Baboon

Roundworm

NEMATODA

VERTEBRATA

Herring

PLATYHELMINTHES

Jellyfish

COELENTERATA

PORIFERA

Flatworm

Sponge

Shark

PROTOZOA

Lamprey

THE WORLD OF ANIMALS

Animals can be found everywhere on Earth, from the deepest ocean floors to the tops of the highest mountains. In all, there are probably well over a million different kinds, each adapted for a particular way of life. Some wriggle through the soil, many crawl or walk on the land, others swim in the seas and in fresh water, while some fly freely through the air.

Animal Groups: Feeding Habits

If animals are grouped according to their main sources of food there are three major groups. These are the carnivores (flesh-eaters), the herbivores (plant-eaters), and the omnivores. (The last group eats both plant and animal material.) During their long history, the animals have explored every possible source of food, and between them the three groups eat just about every kind of plant and animal matter, both living and dead. Insects eat some very strange materials, including cork, wood, tobacco, dung, and bones. Some birds and mammals also eat bones, and quite a number of animals, feed on blood.

The teeth and other feeding equipment are admirably suited to the various diets. We might not be too happy to give blood to a mosquito, but the tiny hollow needle that it has for a mouth is an excellent sucking instrument. On a larger scale, the teeth of the horse are good for biting through tufts of grass and grinding the blades to pulp. The beaks of birds are also closely linked with diet. Insect-eaters, such as wrens, have very slender beaks with which they can pick up very small prey. Seed-eaters have stouter and more powerful beaks to crack open the seeds.

Animal Groups: Body Structures

Grouping animals according to their feeding habits is fine for studying behaviour, but the scientific classification of animals is done by their basic structure. On this system, there are about 30 major groups, called **phyla.** Some of the most important phyla are shown on the opposite page. All the animals in one **phylum** share a number of basic features. All the arthropods, for example, have fairly tough body coverings called exoskeletons, and they all have jointed limbs. All the animals with backbones belong to a group called **vertebrates.** Thus, the baboon is more closely related to the herring, which also has a backbone, than to the crab, which does not. The animals without backbones belong to several phyla, but they are all known as **invertebrates.**

Simple Animals

The simplest animals belong to the phylum known as the **Protozoa.** The world's very first animals were probably similar to some of today's **protozoans.** Each animal consists of just one tiny cell, and the largest ones are little bigger than the full stops on this page. Despite their small size, these tiny creatures are able to carry out all the essential processes of life. Each little cell can breathe, feed, move about, and reproduce itself. These processes are all controlled by the 'brain' of the cell, known as the **nucleus,** which sends chemical messages to all parts.

Complex Animals

Larger animals' bodies consist of many cells—our own bodies contain many millions of cells. These cells are of several different kinds, and each type does a particular job. Plants are also made up of cells.

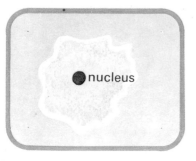

nucleus

Above: The amoeba is a very simple animal. It usually reproduces simply by splitting into two halves. The nucleus or 'brain' splits into two as well.

Below: Butterflies, in common with many other insects, pass through four distinct stages during their lives. The caterpillar that comes out of the egg is very different from the adult, and it also chews leaves. It turns into the adult inside the chrysalis.

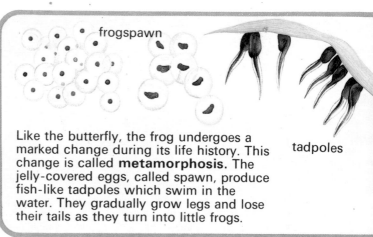

frogspawn

tadpoles

Like the butterfly, the frog undergoes a marked change during its life history. This change is called **metamorphosis.** The jelly-covered eggs, called spawn, produce fish-like tadpoles which swim in the water. They gradually grow legs and lose their tails as they turn into little frogs.

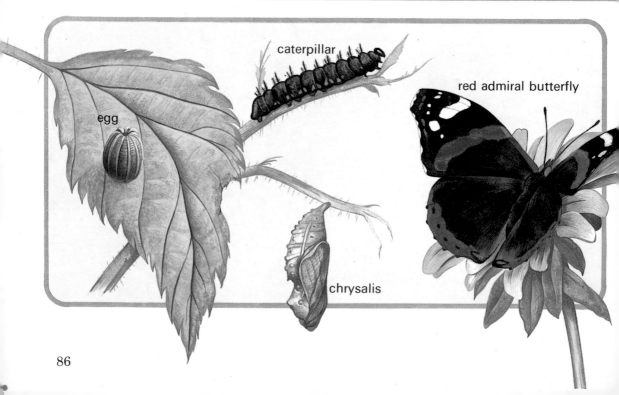

caterpillar

red admiral butterfly

egg

chrysalis

The Next Generation

Reproduction—the production of more of their kind—is something all living things do. In its simplest form, known as asexual reproduction, the animal merely splits into two halves and each half becomes a new individual. Sexual reproduction occurs in most animals. It involves the joining of two special cells, one from each parent. Having joined together, these two cells begin to multiply and they grow into a new animal.

The early stages of growth may take place inside the mother's body, or they may take place inside an egg which the mother lays in a suitable place.

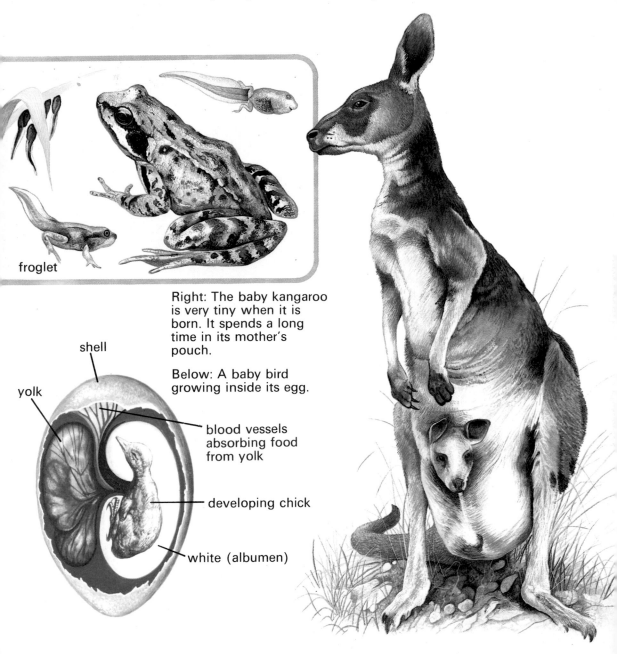

froglet

Right: The baby kangaroo is very tiny when it is born. It spends a long time in its mother's pouch.

Below: A baby bird growing inside its egg.

shell

yolk

blood vessels absorbing food from yolk

developing chick

white (albumen)

A trapdoor spider, with its prey.

Animals without Backbones

Animals without backbones are called **invertebrates.** All of the major groups of invertebrate animals have some water-living members. Some groups are entirely confined to the water. Examples include the jellyfish group (**Coelenterates**) and the starfish group (**Echinoderms**). The latter are found in the seas. The squids, cuttlefishes, and octopuses are also

The razor shell digs itself into the sand until it is completely hidden.

The starfish opens shells with the suckers on its arms.

Cockles move slowly through the sand.

The lugworm swallows mud and sand and digests food in it. The mud is passed out to form casts.

The fiddler crab's large claw is just for show.

Sea slugs have gaudy colours and strange shapes.

Animals living on sandy beaches seek safety by burrowing. This protects them from the force of the waves when the tide is in. Hidden in the sand, the animals are also safe from seagulls when the tide is out, and they do not risk drying up.

A sea cucumber, a member of the starfish group.

Piddocks use their shells to drill into rocks.

confined to the seas, although other members of their group (the **Molluscs**) live on land and in fresh water. The bivalve molluscs, which are those whose shells are in two parts, are confined to water because of the way in which they feed (see below).

Among the many invertebrate animals that live on land are earthworms, centi-pedes, millipedes, slugs and snails, wood-lice, scorpions, spiders, and insects. Many of these still have to live in damp places because they do not have water-proof coats. They come out to feed at night, when the air is damp. Insects, spiders and scorpions have waterproof coats and many can live in extremely dry places, including the hot, dry deserts.

Animals living high up on a rocky shore are exposed to the air for much of the time. The tough shells of limpets and periwinkles prevent them from drying up.

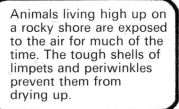

Limpets clamp themselves to rocks.

Periwinkles shelter in damp cracks and under seaweeds when the tide is out.

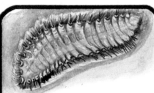

The sand-dwelling sea-mouse is a kind of worm.

Sea-shore animals do not live just anywhere on the beach. They live in distinct zones, according to the amount of exposure they can stand. Periwinkles can survive for many hours out of water, and they live high up on the rocks.

The cuttlefish lives on the sea bed and eats shrimps.

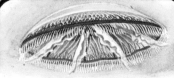

Jellyfishes often sting their prey to death.

Filter-Feeding

Bivalve molluscs, such as the cockles, mussels, and razor shells, feed by straining tiny food particles from the water. Cockles and razor shells are often completely buried when they are feeding. They push tubes, called siphons, to the surface of the sand and suck water in through one of them. Food particles are filtered out as the water passes through the body, and the water then passes out through the other siphon.

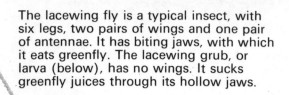

The lacewing fly is a typical insect, with six legs, two pairs of wings and one pair of antennae. It has biting jaws, with which it eats greenfly. The lacewing grub, or larva (below), has no wings. It sucks greenfly juices through its hollow jaws.

THE INSECTS

The insects are the most numerous of all animals. Nearly a million different kinds have already been discovered. They show an enormous variation in shape and size, but an adult insect is very easy to recognize. Its body is always divided into three parts, known as the head, thorax, and abdomen. The head carries a pair of antennae, or feelers, which are used for picking up scent and sound. These are usually hair-like or feathery, but are sometimes like little clubs. There are usually two compound eyes, made up of many tiny lenses. Different insects have different kinds of mouths, according to what they eat. Many have biting jaws to chew solid food, while others have mouths like drinking straws, or like hollow needles, with which they suck up liquid food.

The thorax carries three pairs of legs. It also bears wings in most insects. Bluebottles and other flies have only two wings, but most insects have four. Beetles and many bugs seem wingless at first sight because their front wings are hard and act as shields for the body. The delicate hind wings are folded beneath them. Some primitive insects, such as the silverfish, have no wings at all. Fleas and lice are also wingless. These insects live on the bodies of birds and mammals and suck blood.

Most insects start life as eggs. The baby insects that hatch out have no wings and often look very different from the adults. Butterflies, for example, go through a caterpillar stage (see page 86), and young bluebottles are maggots. The big change to the adult state takes place in the pupa, or chrysalis. Young earwigs and grass-hoppers, on the other hand, resemble the adults quite closely. They gradually acquire wings as they grow up.

The praying mantis spots its prey with its great eyes, catches it with spiky front legs, and chews it with powerful jaws.

The scorpion fly has two pairs of narrow wings and is harmless.

This mayfly has only one pair of wings. Most species have two pairs.

The flea is quite wingless. Wings would be a hindrance to this fur-dwelling parasite.

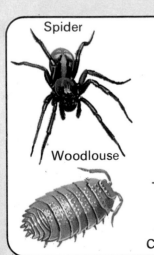

A hand lens magnifying ten times is useful for studying insects. You can draw insects by using three ovals.

Some earwigs have wings but usually keep them folded away out of sight.

Other Arthropods

The animals shown here are often called insects, but they are not insects. They all have jointed legs, and they belong to the same major group as the insects (the arthropods), but they all have more than three pairs of legs. None of them ever has any wings.

Spider

Scorpion

Woodlouse

Millipede

Centipede

The humming-bird hawkmoth hovers in front of flowers and sucks out the nectar with its long tongue. At the same time, it picks up pollen which it later carries to other flowers. This pollinating activity is carried out by many insects and is of vital importance to the plants.

Insects and Humans

Many insects are useful to us. Certain species are eaten in some parts of the world, but most are valuable because they provide us with some useful materials. Silkworms, which are the caterpillars of a moth, provide us with silk, and several kinds of insect yield dyes, such as the cochineal used in food colourings. Honey bees provide us with both honey and bees' wax. Even more important than these products, however, are the pollinating activities of the various kinds of bees. Without bees to carry pollen from flower to flower, we would not get our crops of apples and many other fruits.

Destructive Insects

With so many different kinds of insects eating almost every kind of material, it is not surprising that many of them come into conflict with people. Many of them eat and destroy food and crops; some eat the wood with which we build our houses; others attack us or our domestic animals,

often spreading diseases as they feed. These insects destroy millions of pounds worth of food every year. Familiar crop pests include the cabbage white butterfly and the various kinds of greenfly and

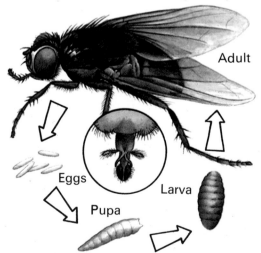

Houseflies lay their eggs in decaying matter. The life cycle can be complete in a week in warm weather. The fly has a sponge-like mouth (shown in the circle) with which it mops up liquid food.

blackfly. The latter are aphids, and they form dense clusters on the leaves and tender shoots of many kinds of plants. They suck the sap and weaken the plants, and they also spread serious virus diseases from plant to plant. Another infamous pest is the Colorado beetle, which is a serious threat to potato crops in many countries.

Thousands of people and domestic animals die from diseases carried by insects. The main human diseases are malaria and yellow fever, both carried by mosquitos, and sleeping sickness which is carried by tsetse-flies in Africa. Lice can carry typhus fever, while fleas can transmit plague. Rabbit fleas carry myxomatosis.

Controlling Insect Pests

The main method of controlling the pests involves the use of poisons called insecticides. These can be sprayed on to crops or stored grain to kill the pests. Timber, clothes, and carpets can also be treated to kill beetles and clothes moths that land on them. Another method, known as biological control, involves releasing the pest's natural enemies to keep its numbers down.

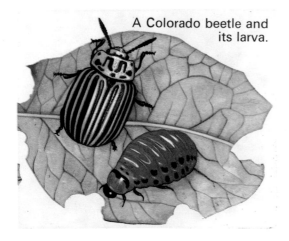

A Colorado beetle and its larva.

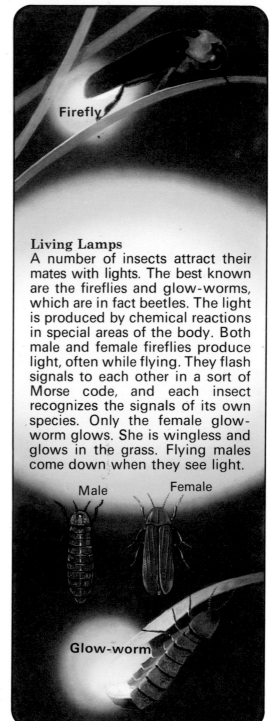

Firefly

Living Lamps

A number of insects attract their mates with lights. The best known are the fireflies and glow-worms, which are in fact beetles. The light is produced by chemical reactions in special areas of the body. Both male and female fireflies produce light, often while flying. They flash signals to each other in a sort of Morse code, and each insect recognizes the signals of its own species. Only the female glow-worm glows. She is wingless and glows in the grass. Flying males come down when they see light.

Male   Female

Glow-worm

Dogfish

Hammerhead shark

Skate

Ray

Rudd

Carp

Pike

Stickleback

Eel

Minnow

THE FISHES

The fishes were the first animals with backbones on Earth. The early forms, many of them without jaws, have long since become extinct, but there are about 20,000 species alive today. About 5,000 of these live in fresh water and the rest are found in the seas. Almost all have scale-covered bodies, and they generally have two pairs of fins which correspond to the limbs of land-living vertebrates. These paired fins are generally concerned with steering and braking. The tail fin provides the driving force as the body moves from side to side in the water. The other fins provide stability.

Bones and Cartilage

The two main groups of fishes are the bony fishes and the **cartilaginous** fishes.

The latter, which include the sharks and rays, have relatively soft skeletons made of cartilage, although their scales are sharp and bony. Their fins are covered with thick, leathery skin. The bony fishes have much more delicate fins, consisting of thin membranes supported on frameworks of stiff or soft spines.

The majority of fishes are very well streamlined for easy passage through the water, but there are some notable exceptions. The plaice and sole, for example, belong to a group known as flatfishes. Their bodies are extremely flattened from side to side and they spend most of their time lying on one side on the sea bed. Skates and rays also live on the sea bed. They are flattened from top to bottom.

Oxygen from the Water

With a few exceptions, the fishes get all

94

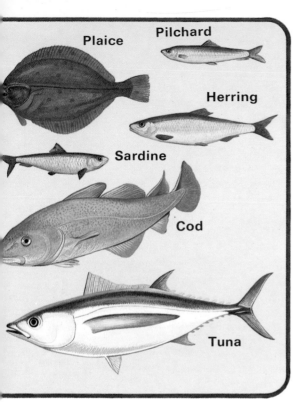

Plaice

Pilchard

Herring

Sardine

Cod

Tuna

Above, there are many different sorts of fishes. On the left are some freshwater fish and on the right, fish that live in the sea.

their oxygen direct from the water through their gills. These are rather feathery organs in the fish's throat region. They are full of tiny blood vessels and they are covered with very thin skin. A fish is continually taking in mouthfuls of water and forcing it over the gills. Oxygen from the water passes into the blood in the gills and is then carried round the body. The water escapes through the gill slits on the sides of the body. Sharks have five slits on each side, but the slits are covered by a flap among the bony fishes and there appears to be only one opening on each side.

THE AMPHIBIANS

The name amphibian means 'double life' and refers to the fact that most of these animals spend part of their lives on land and part in the water. All have thin skins and cannot survive in really dry places. The best known amphibians are the frogs, toads and newts.

The frogs and toads are jumping creatures with long back legs. Many toads have warty skins, but there is no easy way to distinguish the two groups. The animals generally spend their adult lives on land, feeding on slugs, insects, and other small creatures. Most species return to the water to breed. They lay their eggs in jelly-like masses or strings, and the eggs produce fish-like tadpoles. The tadpoles breathe through gills at first, but they eventually develop lungs and legs and turn into little frogs or toads which can leave the water.

Newts are more fish-like than the frogs and toads, for they keep their tails throughout their lives.

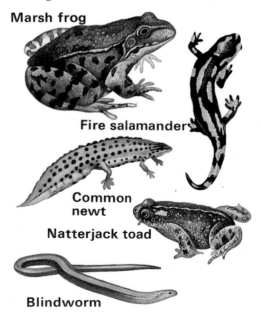

Marsh frog

Fire salamander

Common newt

Natterjack toad

Blindworm

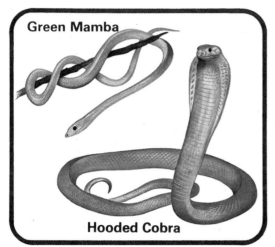

Green Mamba

Hooded Cobra

Snakes, such as the green mamba and the hooded cobra, are cold-blooded (their body temperatures match their surroundings). The mamba and the cobra are among the most poisonous snakes in the world.

THE REPTILES

Reptiles, like fishes and amphibians, are cold-blooded animals with backbones. 'Cold-blooded' means that their body temperature varies with that of the surroundings. Many of them like to bask in the sunshine, and they often have to warm themselves like this before they can be fully active.

Almost all reptiles are covered with scales. Many live in water, but they never have gills for breathing and they have to come up for air. The young look just like their parents. They do not go through a change like amphibians.

There are four major groups of living reptiles: the tortoises and turtles, the crocodiles and alligators, the lizards,

Marine turtles come ashore to lay their eggs in the sand. On hatching, the young turtles struggle to the surface and make for the water, but few get there. Most are eaten by gulls and other birds and by many other predators.

and the snakes. There are about 6,000 species in all, some 3,000 of these being lizards and about 2,600 being snakes. The great majority of them live in tropical regions where there is no problem with warmth, but one snake (the viper) and one lizard (the viviparous lizard) extend into the Arctic Circle. Reptiles living in cool regions hibernate in autumn.

The tortoises and lizards include both plant-eating and flesh-eating species, but the snakes and crocodiles are all flesh-eaters. Snakes have very loosely hinged jaws which enable them to swallow prey much fatter than themselves.

The Nile crocodile is often seen with Egyptian plovers that remove leeches from its skin.

THE BIRDS

The goldfinch has a stout, seed-eating beak, although it eats rather softer seeds than many other finches.

A Coat of Feathers
Feathers are made of horny material called keratin and are thought to have developed from the scales of the ancestral reptiles. Contour feathers, which form the outer coat of the bird, consist of a central shaft and hundreds of interlocking barbs. Underneath them are down feathers which keep the bird warm.

It is impossible to mistake the birds for anything else, because they are the only animals with feathers. In common with the mammals, the birds are warm-blooded creatures. This means that they can keep their bodies at a high temperature even when the surroundings are cold. At first feathers were probably used just for warmth. They would have developed for flight later on in bird history. It is thought that the birds are descended from some kind of tree-living reptile whose front legs gradually became changed into wings. Most of today's birds fly well, but many spend much of their time on the ground and some, such as the ostrich and the kiwi, have lost the power of flight altogether.

No living bird has any teeth, and the jaws are covered with a horny beak instead. The beak is usually used for catching or collecting food as well as for tearing or crushing it, and the shape of the beak varies according to the diet of the bird. Seed-eating birds, for example, tend to have short, stout beaks for crushing the seeds, while hawks and

How a Bird Flies

A bird's wings hold it up in the air as well as producing the thrust to push it forward. Lift is produced as a result of the arched upper surface of the wings. The air is 'stretched out' as it flows over this surface, and the pressure is therefore reduced: upward pressure on the lower wing surface pushes the bird upwards. The downbeat of the wing is the power stroke, during which the wing-tips twist and push air backwards. This pushes the bird forwards. The feathers are separated on the upstroke to reduce air resistance. The wings are held back and the tail is spread to form air-brakes on landing.

other birds of prey have hooked beaks for tearing flesh. The birds' feet also tell us a good deal about their habits—whether they run on the ground, swim, or perch in the trees, for example.

Courtship and Nesting

The males of many bird species attract their mates by their distinctive calls and songs. Many also employ courtship dances, displaying their fine plumage which is often much more colourful than that of the females. Having found mates, the birds prepare for egg-laying. No bird gives birth to active young, for birds have to be as light as possible and carrying developing babies in their body would seriously hinder flight. The eggs are usually laid in nests. Some nests are just hollows in the ground. Others are very complicated, built of twigs, grass, hair, and other materials. The nest may be built by one or both parents, according to the species. Some baby birds, such as ducks, can feed themselves as soon as they come out of the eggs. Others are naked and helpless, and have to be cared for by their parents for several weeks.

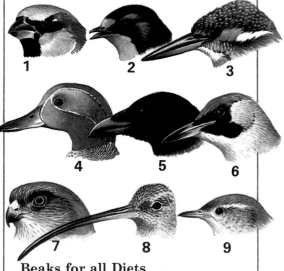

Beaks for all Diets

Birds' beaks vary enormously with diet. 1. House sparrow (cracking seeds) 2. Swallow (wide gape for flying insects) 3. Kingfisher (fish) 4. Duck (straining food from water) 5. Crow (all-purpose) 6. Woodpecker (probing bark) 7. Sparrowhawk (flesh) 8. Curlew (probing mud) 9. Wren (insects)

WOODLAND BIRDS

Long-eared Owl

Crested Tit

Coal Tit

Goldcrest

Capercaillie

Crossbill

Nightingale

Woodpigeon

Green Woodpecker

Lesser Spotted Woodpecker

Bullfinch

Sparrowhawk

Treecreeper

Blackcap

Chiffchaff

Great Tit

COASTAL BIRDS

Common Gull

Herring Gull

Lesser Black-backed Gull

Common Tern

Little Tern

Cormorant

Oystercatcher

Gannet

Guillemot

Razorbill

Puffin

BIRDS OF PONDS AND STREAMS

Kingfisher

male
female
Mallard

Pochard

Shoveler

female
male
Tufted Duck

Greylag Goose

Pintail

Grey Heron

Mute Swan

Reed Warbler

Water Rail

BIRDS OF THE FIELD

Cuckoo

Yellowhammer

Skylark

Yellow Wagtail

Red-backed Shrike

Whitethroat

Redwing

Fieldfare

Goldfinch

Lapwing

Pheasant

Quail

Partridge

Female Pheasant

UPLAND BIRDS

Buzzard

Raven

Golden Eagle

Ptarmigan

Black Grouse

Willow Grouse

Wheatear

Dipper

Meadow Pipit

TOWN BIRDS

Mistle Thrush

Blackbird

Long-tailed Tit

Blue Tit

Dunnock

Greenfinch

Starling

Wren

Robin

House Martin

Feral Pigeon

Collared Dove

Pied Wagtail

Carrion Crow

Magpie

Rook

THE MAMMALS

All mammals have some things in common. They are all warm-blooded, they have backbones, and they all feed their babies on milk from the mother's body.

Bats

These animals are the only mammals that can really fly. Their wings consist of webs of skin supported on the long fingers of the front legs and running back to the hind legs and the tail. Most bats fly at night and catch insects with the aid of remarkable radar systems. They send out high-pitched sounds, and pick up the echoes bouncing back from flying insects. The insects are crunched up by numerous sharp teeth. The insect-eating bats sleep through the winter in cool climates where there are few insects. Some large tropical bats eat fruit. They are often called flying foxes because their faces are very fox-like. A few bats snatch fishes from the water surface, while the infamous vampires bite other animals and

A bat in flight

drink their blood. The female bat generally gives birth to just one baby at a time.

Bats belong to a group by themselves. The group name is **chiroptera.**

Insect-Eaters

These are all rather small mammals with lots of sharp teeth. The best known are the moles, hedgehogs, and shrews. Although they are called insect-eaters (the group name is **insectivores**), the animals eat many things apart from insects. Earthworms are the main food of the mole, which lives almost entirely under the ground. Hedgehogs also like worms, as well as slugs and fruit. The hedgehog's spines are stiff hairs and they protect it from most of its enemies. These animals are rarely active by day. The shrews are mouse-like animals, but they have much longer and more pointed snouts than mice. They have to eat large quantities of food to keep alive and, apart from several short rest periods, they are active all day and all night. Insects and slugs are their main foods. The Etruscan shrew from southern Europe is no more than about 50 mm long (excluding tail).

A hedgehog

The Aardvark

The aardvark is a group all by itself! It is called a **tubulidentata.** It has a pig-like body with a thick tail, large ears, and a long snout. It uses its strong legs and claws to break open the nests of ants and termites, and then it plunges its long, sticky tongue into the nests to scoop up the insects.

Rodents

The rodents are the largest group of mammals, with about 3,000 out of a total of little over 4,500 species. They include rats, mice, voles, squirrels, beavers, guinea-pigs, and porcupines. The largest rodent is the capybara, a pig-sized relative of the guinea-pig which lives in South America. The rodent group name is **rodentia.**

The rodents are all gnawing mammals, with large, chisel-shaped front teeth.

These teeth have a very hard coat of orange enamel at the front and they can cut through some of the toughest materials. A beaver, for example, can fell a 15 cm-diameter tree with its teeth in just three minutes. It feeds on the nutritious inner bark, and also uses the timber to make its home. The rodents are all basically vegetarians, although some mice and voles eat plenty of insects and other small animals. Rats and house mice are real scavengers, eating anything they can find. Seeds and grasses are the main foods of most species.

There are no rodents in the seas, but these animals can be found almost everywhere else, including some of the hottest and coldest places on Earth. Lemmings and various voles continue to forage under the Arctic snow, while jerboas and kangaroo rats live in hot deserts and manage to survive on dry seeds without ever taking a drink.

A dormouse—one of the few rodents that go to sleep for the winter

A red squirrel gnawing a cone to get at the seeds

The beaver's flat tail is a useful building tool.

A tamandua—a tree-living ant-eater—and its baby

American Oddities

There is a strange group of animals, called **edentates,** found only in South and Central America. They include the armadillos, the ant-eaters, and the sloths. Armadillos are short-legged, barrel-like creatures that are protected by several bony plates on their backs. There are about 20 species, living in both forest and grassland and ranging from 15 cm to one metre in length. Many of them live in burrows. They eat both plant and animal food, but concentrate on ants and termites.

Ant-eaters have no teeth and feed almost entirely on ants and termites. They rip open the nests with their strong claws, poke in their long snouts, and mop up the insects with their sticky tongues. The silky ant-eater and the tamandua live in the trees, while the giant ant-eater roams the grassland.

Sloths are slow-moving forest animals that spend a lot of time hanging upside down by their great claws. They eat fruit and leaves. There are three species in tropical America.

One- or three-toed Mammals

Hoofed mammals which generally have one or three toes on each foot are called **perissodactyla.** The horses, zebras, and asses make up one group. All are fast-running animals of the plains, with long legs and just one large toe and hoof on each foot. They usually live in small herds or family groups.

The rhinoceroses form another group of perissodactyls. They have three toes on each foot. There are five living species —the Indian, Javan, and Sumatran rhinos from Asia, and the black and white rhinos from Africa. The white rhino reaches weights of about 4 tonnes and, apart from the elephants, it is the largest living land animal. Rhinoceroses browse or graze in the forests and the grasslands. They have either one or two horns on their noses.

The tapirs form the third group of perissodactyls. They have three toes on their hind feet and four on the front. The two species live in the forests of South America and South-East Asia.

Many breeds of horse exist today, each bred for a different job

A red stag displays his antlers, which he uses to fight other stags at breeding time

Two- or four-toed Mammals

Hoofed mammals that have an even number of toes—either two or four—on each foot are sometimes called cloven-hoofed. They belong to the **artiodactyla** group. There are almost 200 species, including pigs, hippopotamuses, camels, deer, giraffes, antelopes, cattle, sheep, and goats. Apart from the pigs, which are scavengers, they are all grazing and browsing animals, feeding on grasses and other plants. Nearly all bolt their food down into special stomachs and then bring it up again later to be chewed properly. This is called chewing the cud.

Artiodactyls inhabit forest, grassland, and mountain and often live in large herds. Many species carry horns, which are generally larger in the male. The female may have no horns at all. The horns may be straight or curved, but never branched. The branched antlers of deer are made of solid bone. Female reindeer have antlers, but otherwise they are found only on the male.

Lagomorpha

The animals in this group are the hares and rabbits and their mountain-dwelling relatives called pikas. They have gnawing front teeth similar to those of the rodents, but there is a second and much smaller pair of teeth just behind the upper front ones. The animals feed mainly on grasses and other low-growing plants.

Hares and rabbits both have long ears and look rather alike, but hares have longer ears and longer legs. Hares bound away when disturbed, while the rabbits merely scuttle. Hares, often known as jack-rabbits in America, give birth to fully-furred babies which have their eyes open and which can run about almost straight away. Rabbits, which are known as cottontails in America, give birth to blind, naked, and helpless babies. Those of the European rabbit are born in deep burrows. Cottontails are born in small hollows lined with the mother's fur.

A family of rabbits

Meat Eaters

This group of mammals, called **carnivores,** are all hunters and killers. They include the cats, dogs, weasels, otters, badgers, mongooses, raccoons, and hyenas. The bears also belong to the group, although, with the exception of the polar bear, they eat more plant material than animal food. The fish-eating seals and sea-lions are close relatives of the meat eaters.

This group of animals all have large canines, or eye teeth, with which they stab and tear their prey. The teeth can be seen very easily when a cat yawns. The cheek teeth have sharp edges for shearing through the meat.

The animals hunt and catch their prey in many different ways. Some, such as the cheetah, hunt by day, but most of them are active by night. Sight is important for the daytime hunters, while others rely more on picking up scents and sounds. The two major techniques are careful stalking and high-speed chasing. Most cats stalk their prey and pounce on it when they are within range. Wolves and other dogs are built for running, and they usually chase their prey over long distances. Hyenas also chase, and, like the wolves and hunting dogs, they generally improve their chances by hunting in groups.

The babies are generally born in a helpless state and they have to spend a long time with their mothers, and often with their fathers as well. During this period the youngsters play with each other and gradually learn the hunting and tracking skills that they will need when they grow up.

Foxes (below) and badgers (far right) are Britain's largest carnivores. Both live in burrows and often share one tunnel system. Both like eating rabbits. The fox scatters bones and feathers around its den.

The blue whale

Whales

The whales are **cetaceans**—stream-lined mammals that have become completely adapted for life in the sea. They include the dolphins and porpoises as well as the much larger species. The blue whale, up to 35 metres long, is the largest animal that has ever lived. The front legs of the whales have been turned into flippers, and the back legs are absent. The large horizontal tail drives the animal through the water. Some whales have teeth and eat large prey, but others have great fringes of baleen, or whale-bone, in their mouths. They use them to sift tonnes of tiny animals (plankton) from the water. The blue whale feeds in this way. Whales are quite unable to leave the water and their babies are born at sea. Because they are mammals, the babies have to surface at once to take in air.

The chimpanzee is man's nearest living relative and is a very intelligent ape. It can use simple tools and readily learns how to unlock doors and boxes.

Primates

The primates include the lemurs, monkeys, apes, and man. The most obvious features of these animals are the forward-looking eyes and the grasping hands—both of supreme importance to animals which are essentially tree-dwellers and spend much of their time leaping about in the branches. An efficient brain is another important feature. Most of the animals eat fruit and insects, but the langur monkeys specialize in eating leaves.

Lemurs are among the most primitive primates and they are found only in Madagascar. They have more prominent snouts than other primates. Bush-babies and tarsiers are related to the lemurs. They are largely nocturnal and have huge eyes.

Monkeys fall into two groups—the New World monkeys of America and the Old World monkeys of Africa and Asia. New World monkeys include spider and howler monkeys and have broad noses. Many have prehensile tails that can be used like a spare hand. Old World monkeys include baboons and macaques and have narrow noses. They never have prehensile tails. Apes have no tails at all. They include the gibbon and orangutan of Asia and the gorilla and chimpanzee of Africa.

Pangolins

Pangolins, or scaly ant-eaters, are the only mammals in the **pholidota** group. The hair on the back has been modified into broad, overlapping scales. There are several species, up to 1.5 m long, in Africa and Asia. They feed on ants and termites, ripping open the nests with their large claws. When frightened, a pangolin rolls into a ball and the tough scales protect it from most of its enemies.

Dugongs and Manatees

The dugong, and three species of manatee, are included in a group called **sirenia.** They live in tropical seas and rivers and browse on seaweeds and other plants. They are often called sea-cows. Although they look like seals, they have no hind legs. They are more closely related to the elephants. Their habit of floating in the water probably gave rise to the idea of mermaids.

Hyraxes

The group name for these rodent-like animals is **hyracoidea.** They are about the size of a rabbit but with very short legs and ears. They have hoof-like nails on their toes and they are actually the nearest living relatives of the elephants. They live in Africa and Arabia and they are also known as conies. Some graze on rocky hillsides, often in large colonies, while others browse in the trees.

Elephants

These mammals are called **proboscideae**, and are the largest living land animals. There are two living species: the African elephant, which lives on the tree-dotted savannas, and the Asiatic elephant which lives in the forests. The African species is the larger, with weights up to 6 tonnes, and it can be recognized by its huge ears (see below). The Asiatic elephant's ears do not reach below its eyes. Both species feed mainly on tree leaves and branches, gathering food with their trunks.

ANIMAL BEHAVIOUR

Animal behaviour is of two main sorts: instinctive and learned. Instinctive behaviour is what the animal is born with, and is part of it, like its shape and colour. The animal automatically knows what to do in a given situation. A spider, for example, knows exactly how to build its web without ever being taught. Learned behaviour is acquired by an animal during its lifetime, usually by watching other animals performing various tasks. A blue-tit, for example, is not born with the knowledge that it can get cream by pecking through milk bottle tops, but by watching other birds it soon learns that this is a good source of food. The behaviour of most insects and other invertebrate animals is entirely instinctive. Birds and mammals employ a good deal of instinctive behaviour, but this is changed to some extent by behaviour learned during their lives.

Most animal behaviour revolves around three major activities: feeding, avoiding enemies, and breeding. Repro-

Different kinds of animals often form close associations for their mutual benefit. Oxpeckers perch on large animals, such as this rhinoceros, and peck ticks from their skins. Egrets eat insects stirred up by the animals' hooves. Both kinds of birds also warn the mammals of approaching danger, by flying away.

duction is not essential for an individual, but it is of vital importance to the species as a whole. If the animals do not produce offspring, the whole species will die out. Animals therefore have very strong instinctive urges to find mates.

Courtship and Mating

Most animal species have two distinct sexes, the male and the female. They can breed only when the two sexes meet. Various forms of courtship behaviour are used to bring the sexes together. Among the best-known examples are the songs of birds, normally performed by the males to attract the females. Many birds also attract and encourage the females by displaying colourful plumage. Male birds of paradise, for example, put on elaborate dances and display some of the finest feathers in the world. Male newts and

many fish also indulge in colourful courtship dances, while female mammals generally use scent to attract and stimulate the males.

Having paired up, the animals may indulge in further courtship displays, such as dancing and 'kissing', before they mate. During mating, the male releases his sperm, which joins with the female's eggs. This is called fertilization, and it may take place inside or outside the female's body. The fertilized eggs grow into new animals. This development takes place inside the female's body among the mammals and certain other animals, but otherwise the female lays her eggs and development continues outside her body. The birds and a few other animals, including some fish, look after their eggs, but most eggs are abandoned to hatch on their own.

This ant nest consists of a maze of tunnels and chambers. Eggs are cared for in some, larvae are fed in others, and pupae tended in others. Some chambers are used as food stores, and even as cemeteries.

Ruby-throated Humming-bird

Golden oriole

Long-tailed tit

Woodpecker

Tailor bird

Wren

Sand martin nests in cliff-face tunnels

Ringed plover

Nests and Homes

Many animals wander about freely through their surroundings, and have no settled home. They sleep wherever they happen to be each day. Other animals keep to a fairly distinct area, or territory, and may have a definite sleeping place to which they return every day. The sleeping quarters may be nothing more than a hollow under a stone, such as is used by a toad or a snail, or they may be very elaborate constructions like the burrows of badgers and rabbits and the nests of birds.

Birds' nests are actually much more like nurseries than homes, for they are used almost exclusively for rearing the young. With a few exceptions, the nests are abandoned when the youngsters have flown. New nests are usually built for the next breeding season, although some birds, such as the house martin, often return and repair their old nests. Some of the amazing variety of birds' nests are shown on the opposite page. They vary from the ringed plover's simple scrape in the shingle, to the enclosed nursery of the long-tailed tit and the fascinating construction of the tailor bird. This bird from South East Asia makes its nest by sewing leaves together with roots and fibres.

Nest-building may be carried out by one or both sexes and it is almost entirely instinctive. Courtship behaviour combined with internal urges causes the birds to begin their nests, and each stage of building seems to trigger off the next stage automatically.

Permanent homes are built by various mammals, and by some insects. Among the latter, the best known are the ants and termites. These are all social insects and their nests may contain upwards of a million individuals. Termites often build huge mounds, full of 'rooms' in which the youngsters are fed and cared for and in which food is stored. Some termite species even grow crops of fungi in their nests, and an elaborate system of tunnels ensures a good circulation of air. The insects, in fact, build air-conditioning systems.

Rabbits, moles, and badgers all dig burrows, but the most elaborate mammal homes are built by rodents. Most are in the form of cosy, grass-lined burrows, but the supreme example is the beaver's lodge (seen below). Built by a family of beavers, the lodge is a masterpiece of engineering consisting of mud, stones, and branches rising up from the bed of a pond. The entrances are underwater, but the living room is above water level and well ventilated by a 'chimney' rising through the centre.

The Beaver's Lodge

Ventilation chimney

Living room

Adult beaver entering through underwater tunnel with a baby beaver

SURVIVAL

Life is a never-ending struggle between animals and their enemies and, over thousands of generations, the hunted animals have evolved numerous features and habits that help them to survive. Defensive weapons include the horns and hooves of various mammals and the spines of the hedgehogs and porcupines.

The stings of bees and ants are chemical weapons which produce their effect by injecting poison into the enemy. The skunk and the bombardier beetle actually fire repulsive liquids at their enemies, and many other animals have acquired unpleasant tastes which ensure that they are left alone. Examples include ladybirds and various brightly coloured frogs. The bright colours warn enemies of the

The musk oxen of the far north have to defend themselves against the cold as well as against wolves and other enemies. Dense, long hair keeps out the cold, while the animals' great horns are a good defence against the marauding wolves.

When attacked by wolves, the musk oxen form a circle facing outwards. No wolf can get through the ring of horns to reach the young musk oxen sheltering safely in the centre of the circle.

unpleasant taste. Speed is another very important attribute of the hunted animal, allowing it to out-run its enemies. This is used by most of the antelopes, which bound away as soon as they see lions or other hunters within a certain dangerous distance.

Concealment is a very important survival technique, especially among the invertebrate animals. It involves various forms of camouflage through which the animals escape the notice of their enemies. Many moths and caterpillars, for example, blend in beautifully with their backgrounds and are very difficult to see because their colours match so well. Other caterpillars, stick insects, and various other insects actually resemble twigs and leaves and may be even more difficult to detect. Some of these fascinating examples are illustrated on this page.

Not all animals manage to evade or escape from their enemies, even if they do have efficient defences, because the predators also evolve more efficient behaviour to help them catch their prey. The struggle for survival is thus a continuing process, with the hunted animals always trying to remain one step ahead of the hunters.

1. Katydid mimicking lichen.
2. Purple thorn moth caterpillar mimicking a twig.
3. Treble bar moth on tree bark.
4. Leaf bug.
5. Thorn tree hoppers look like thorns.
6. Stick insect.

119

ANIMAL JOURNEYS

When it is summer in the northern parts of the world, it is winter in the southern hemisphere. As winter comes to the north, the southern lands begin to feel the warmth of spring. Many animals avoid these seasonal changes, and escape winter altogether, by making long journeys between the northern and southern hemispheres. These journeys are called migrations, and some of the best-known and farthest-reaching travellers are to be found among the birds.

Swallows are sun-loving, insect-eating birds. They arrive in northern regions in late spring and build their nests. There are plenty of insects for them to catch as they sweep gracefully through the air. When winter comes, most of the flying insects are dead. The swallows would die

Migration routes of swallows from Africa to Europe. The birds cover thousands of kilometres in a few weeks.

Swallow

EUROPE

A bullfinch watches the swallows depart

as well if they stayed in the north, but they move on before the food runs out. As the days grow shorter in the autumn, the swallows gather together. You sometimes see hundreds of them perching on telephone wires. When the right moment comes, they begin to fly south.

European swallows cross the Mediterranean Sea and the Sahara Desert, and end up on the warm plains all over the southern half of Africa. They stay there for several months, feeding on the abundant insects while Europe shivers its way through the winter. Then the birds begin the long journey back to the cooler lands of the north, where they lay their eggs and bring up their young. The swallows of America undertake similar migrations between the northern and southern continents.

Other well known migratory birds include the European cuckoo, the swift and the house martin, the turtle dove, and many warblers. These all come north for the summer, but there are also winter visitors. These include many ducks and geese that breed in the far north. They fly south to avoid the severe northern

Migration routes of swallows from Europe to Africa. The birds choose the shortest sea crossings.

AFRICA

A carmine bee-eater watches the swallows arrive

winter. They cannot find food in the north when all the rivers and lakes are frozen.

Birds are not the only animals that migrate. The monarch butterfly is a well-known traveller in North America. It breeds over much of Canada and the United States during the summer, and huge flocks of butterflies then move down to the southern USA and Mexico for the winter. Red admiral and painted lady butterflies make similar, although less spectacular, migrations in Europe.

Mammals also migrate, although on a smaller scale than flying animals. The reindeer, or caribou, move north on the the treeless tundra to graze in summer.

They retreat to the forests in winter. The wolves that prey on them also move in this way. Whales often move into warmer waters to have their babies. Lemmings occasionally indulge in a special form of migration called emigration. When their populations get too high, large numbers leave the area in search of new feeding grounds and they never return. Most of them die.

Navigation by Sun and Compass
Scientists have found out that many birds navigate by the Sun and stars, just as sailors do. Others use the Earth's magnetism, and so do some migratory fishes. Exactly how they manage this astonishing feat of navigation is a mystery, but it seems that their bodies act rather like compass needles.

The bison makes regular migrations over the plains to exploit the best grazing pastures at each season

Antelope herds follow the rains in Africa to find the freshest grasses

Geese generally breed in the far north and fly south when their northern homes become frozen in winter Whooper and Bewick's swans move down from the Arctic in winter like the geese

Long Distance Fliers

The European swallow may cover over 20,000 km each year on its migrations, but some birds fly much farther than this. The white-rumped sandpiper, for example, breeds on the Arctic coasts of Canada and then flies off to spend the southern summer on the beaches of Patagonia. The champion flier, however, is the Arctic tern. It breeds on the Arctic coasts and then flies to the Antarctic. This makes a round trip of over 35,000 km in a year, nearly all of it over featureless oceans.

Swallows migrate in flocks and instinctively know which way to go. Young birds can find their way to Africa even if they are separated from the adults who have done the journey before.

Reindeer eat lichens on the tundra in summer, but move south into the forests for the winter

The monarch, or milkweed, butterfly covers large distances in North America as it spreads northwards in spring

The wolf migrates with the reindeer herds

Norwegian lemmings rush out in all directions when they get too numerous. Many drown as they try to cross rivers

THE WINTER SLEEP

As we have seen on the previous pages, many animals escape the winter cold and food shortage by migrating to warmer lands. Some other animals avoid these problems by going into a deep sleep for the winter. This winter sleep is called hibernation.

Cold-blooded animals, such as reptiles and amphibians, are unable to move about in very cold weather. Their bodies remain at the same temperature as their surroundings, and they get slower and slower as the surroundings cool down. At the onset of autumn, they retire to a snug retreat and stay there until stirred to action by the warmth of spring. Most insects spend the winter in a similar way, although some moths and gnats manage to fly in all but the very coldest weather.

The mammals can keep their bodies at a constant high temperature even in the depths of winter, but they must have plenty of food to do it. Shortage of food is the main reason for hibernation among the mammals. Bats, for example, could not possibly collect enough flying insects in the winter, and they go into hibernation quite early. Dormice hibernate, and thereby avoid competition with voles and squirrels in the winter, when these are searching for nuts. Hedgehogs also hibernate, although the closely-related shrews manage to find enough insects and other small animals to eat.

Before hibernating, the animals store fat in their bodies. When they go to sleep, their body temperature falls drastically and their heart-beat and breathing rate slow right down. Hardly any energy is used up and the fat reserves last them until the spring.

Snake

Stoat

Dormouse

Toad

Tortoise

Above: Bats hibernate in dry caves. Their body temperature may fall so low that dew forms on their fur.

Below: Some hibernating animals in their resting places. Many mammals, such as the stoat and badger, remain active, although the badger does not come out every night. Bears (below right) do not really hibernate, although they sleep for several days at a time.

Badger

Brown bear

Newt

Hedgehog

125

Atkinso

ANIMALS BY NIGHT

Many small animals, including slugs and snails, woodlice, and centipedes, come out at night because they do not have waterproof skins. The air is always more moist at night, and the animals are less likely to dry up and die than they are in the daytime. Hedgehogs, mice, toads, and similar creatures are also active at night. This is because they feed on the smaller nocturnal (night-active) animals. The chain then passes on to a second tier of predators, including foxes, badgers, stoats, and owls. It is less easy to see why animals like rabbits should be active at night, but it may be a way for them to avoid eagles, buzzards, and other large diurnal (day-active) birds of prey.

Moths and many beetles have probably become nocturnal to avoid competition with the hordes of day-flying insects, but they have not escaped enemies. The bats capture them very efficiently. Nightjars also catch large numbers of insects at night. These birds swoop through the air and catch the insects in their wide beaks, just as the swallows catch insects during the daytime.

The owls have extremely good eyesight and can find a mouse on what seems to us a completely black night. They also have amazing hearing, and can detect the slightest rustle in the grass below. Most other nocturnal animals rely on their senses of smell and hearing. The moist night air holds scents much better than the drier air of the day, and this helps both hunter and hunted. Large ears are found in many nocturnal mammals, including the foxes and bats. Bats rely entirely on their ears to pick up echoes from insects and other objects and they quickly change direction to snatch the insects in mid-air.

Owl

Badger

Mouse

The Silent Killers

The owls are supremely suited to capturing small rodents and other animals at night. Their eyes are more efficient than our own. The large 'window' at the front lets in the maximum amount of light, and the round lens produces a bright image. The eyes look forward, like our own, and the owl can judge distances very accurately. It plunges down towards its prey and thrusts out its talons to make the kill. The prey is taken by surprise because the owl flies silently. Delicate fringes on the front edges of the feathers eliminate the noise of air rushing over the wings.

Human eye

Owl's eye

Bat

Fox

Rabbit

Stoat

Hedgehog

THE HUMAN BODY

Our bodies are made of millions of tiny cells. Inside a thin covering of skin and a framework of bones there are all the different parts that allow us to move, breathe, speak, eat and sleep. Our ears, eyes and other senses tell the brain what is going on outside our bodies. The brain controls everything that we do.

All the parts of our bodies work together to make the most perfect machine in the world.

The Skeleton
If you did not have a skeleton you would not be able to stand up! The skeleton is a framework of more than 200 bones, linked by joints. The joints allow us to move, and the bones are held together with stretchy ligaments.

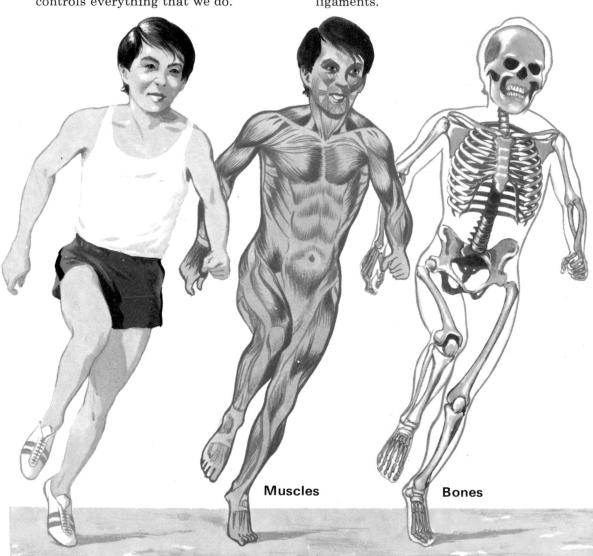

Muscles

Bones

Breathing

The constant and effortless movement of our lungs when we breathe draws a vital supply of oxygen into our bodies. Without this regular supply of oxygen, all our cells would die.

The lungs suck air into the body and blow it out like a pair of bellows. The blood absorbs the oxygen from the lungs and takes it to other parts of the body.

When we breathe out, air passes through a part of the windpipe called the voice box. Cords in the voice box are pulled taut by muscles and as the air passes by them, the cords vibrate and make sounds. We make the sounds into words by moving our lips and tongue.

The Skin

The skin is a waterproof covering that protects the body. It keeps us warm when it is cold, and cool when it is hot. It helps

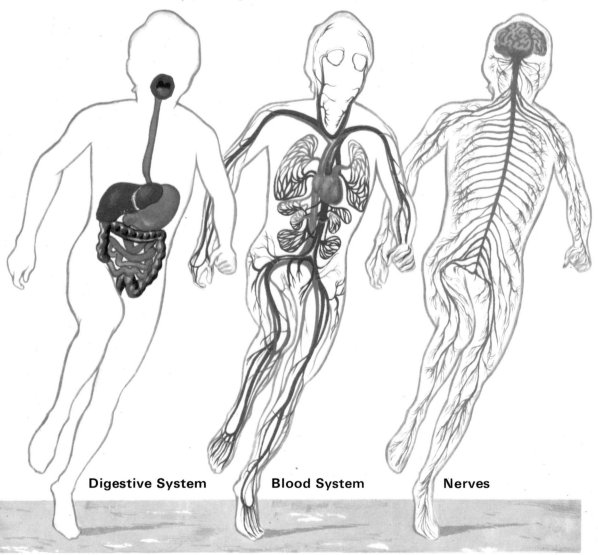

Digestive System   **Blood System**   **Nerves**

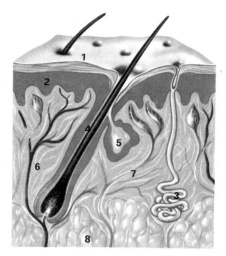

A cutaway of the skin, showing:
1. Surface 2. Epidermis 3. Sweat gland
4. Hair 5. Sebaceous gland 6. Blood
7. Nerve 8. Fat. The nerve endings in the
skin help us to feel cold, heat and pain.

us to get rid of waste water by sweating, and acts as a strong barrier against germs.

The skin is only about one millimetre thick. The outer surface is made of dead cells that flake off all the time. These are too small for us to see. Underneath there are two more layers and some fat.

The layer of skin under the surface has a pattern of ridges and dents which you can see on your finger tips. The pattern you are born with never changes, and no one else in the world has finger-prints exactly like yours.

The Brain and Nerves

The brain is the body's control centre. It is connected to every part of the body by nerves. Messages are carried to and from the brain by the nerves. If it gets too dark for you to read a book, nerves in your eyes will inform your brain. Then the brain will instruct other nerves to tell your muscles to move, so that you can put the light on!

Different parts of the brain control different things such as speaking, hearing and seeing. We use our brains to think, and also to 'store' everything that we know.

Food and Digestion

We get our energy from the food we eat. Our bodies use food as fuel, and from the moment it enters our mouths it is being digested. As the food goes from our mouths and through our stomachs to our intestines, it gets broken down into smaller and smaller pieces. The blood absorbs the food from the intestines and carries it around the body.

Muscles

The joints can only move because they have muscles attached to them, which pull them into the right positions. Muscles work in pairs. To raise the lower part of your arm, one muscle contracts and pulls the bone up, the other muscle is relaxed. To lower your arm the first muscle relaxes and the other one contracts.

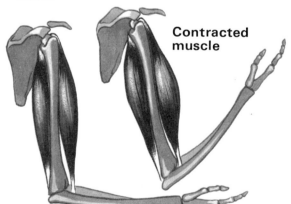

Contracted muscle

The Senses

We know what is going on around us because our senses tell us. We can feel anything that touches our skin and we can see, hear, taste and smell.

Blood

The blood carries oxygen and digested food to all the cells of the body. It carries waste from the cells back to the lungs and to the kidneys. The blood is pumped around the body by the heart. Nearly 5 litres of blood are pumped by the heart every minute. You can feel the blood moving if you hold the pulse in your wrist very tightly with your fingers.

The Eye

The eye is like a very small but accurate camera. The pupil is like the camera's aperture. It enlarges to admit more light or less light, depending on the brightness of our surroundings. The lens and cornea form a focusing aparatus which is like the lens of a camera. Light from the object that we are looking at goes through the lens behind the pupil and throws a picture or image on to the retina at the back of the eye. A large nerve carries the information about the image to the brain and the brain tells us what we are seeing. The image on the back of the eye is always upside down but the brain makes us see it the right way up.

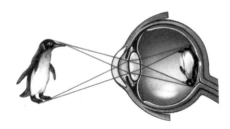

The Ear

Sounds are vibrations in the air and we hear them with our ears. The part of the ear you can see picks up the vibrations and these make the ear drum inside vibrate, just as the skin of an ordinary drum vibrates when you hit it. The vibrations are passed on to three tiny bones. These bang on each other, and pass the vibrations deep inside the ear. There, the vibrations travel around a coiled tube. Tiny nerve cells in the tube pick up the vibration and send signals to the brain. The brain makes sense of the signals and tells us what the sound is. The ear also helps us to keep our balance.

Body Facts

Blood takes about one minute to go from the heart, around the body, and back to the heart again.

The skin covering the body measures almost 2 square metres.

We have between 90,000 and 140,000 hairs on our heads.

The lungs can hold between 3 to 5 litres of air. About half a litre is taken in at each breath.

An average adult drinks about 1.5 litres of liquid and eats about 1.5 kilogrammes of food every day.

If all the blood vessels in a human body were laid end to end they would stretch for nearly 100,000 kilometres.

An adult's brain weighs about 1.5 kilogrammes.

ANIMAL LIFESPANS

	average
Antelope	10
Bear	15–50
Cat	15
Cattle	20
Deer	10–20
Dog	12–15
Donkey	20
Duck	10
Elephant	60
Fox	10
Giraffe	10–25
Goat	10
Goose	25
Hippopotamus	30–40
Horse	20–30
Kangaroo	10–20
Lion	25
Ostrich	50
Pig	10–15
Rabbit	5–8
Rhinoceros	25–50
Sheep	10–15
Tiger	10–25
Whale	20
Zebra	20–25

SPEED IN NATURE

Spine-tailed swift	170 km/h
Sailfish	109 km/h
Cheetah	105 km/h
Pronghorn antelope	97 km/h
Racing pigeon	97 km/h
Lion	80 km/h
Gazelle	80 km/h
Hare	72 km/h
Zebra	64 km/h
Racehorse	64 km/h
Shark	64 km/h
Greyhound	63 km/h
Rabbit	56 km/h
Giraffe	51 km/h
Grizzly bear	48 km/h
Cat	48 km/h
Elephant	40 km/h
Seal	40 km/h
Man	32 km/h
Black Mamba	32 km/h
Bee	18 km/h
Pig	18 km/h
Chicken	14 km/h
Spider	1.88 km/h
Tortoise	0.8 km/h
Snail	0.05 km/h

WORLD POPULATION 'EXPLOSION'

AD	millions (est.)	AD	millions (est.)	AD	millions (est.)
AD1	250	1955	2,713	1975	4,022
1650	550	1960	2,982	1980	4,457
1750	750	1965	3,289	1985	4,933
1800	950	1970	3,632	1990	5,438
1850	1,200	1971	3,706	1995	5,961
1900	1,550	1972	3,782	2000	6,493
1925	1,900	1973	3,860	2070	25,000
1950	2,486	1974	3,950	2100	48,000

World History

HOW OLD IS MANKIND

In 1650, an Irish churchman named Bishop Ussher worked out the date when the world and all its plants, animals and people, were created. From his studies of the Bible, he concluded that life began at 9 am on October 23, 4004 BC.

In fact, the bishop was nowhere near the truth. The world is a much more ancient place than he ever imagined. Signs of very ancient civilizations abound in the Middle East. The ruins of Jericho show that a thriving town existed there as early as 7000 BC. Even a thousand years before that, people in the same region were farming wild grain, and herding cattle, sheep and goats.

Tens of thousands of years before the first civilizations, human beings were already living in small groups. They hunted game and fished, dug for roots, and gathered nuts, berries, fruit and insects. Their tools were made of wood, bone and stone. They used fires, built rough homes, spoke languages and worshipped many different gods.

These prehistoric people, who already looked very much the way we do today, evolved from ape-like ancestors about 100,000 years ago. But the very first signs of human beings are older still; they go back well over two million years.

The Rise of Modern People

Modern-looking human beings spread across the world as the last Ice Age began to draw to a close about 30,000 years ago. Wherever they went, they soon wiped out their more primitive Ice Age ancestors. As the glaciers shrank and retreated, plants, and then grazing animals,

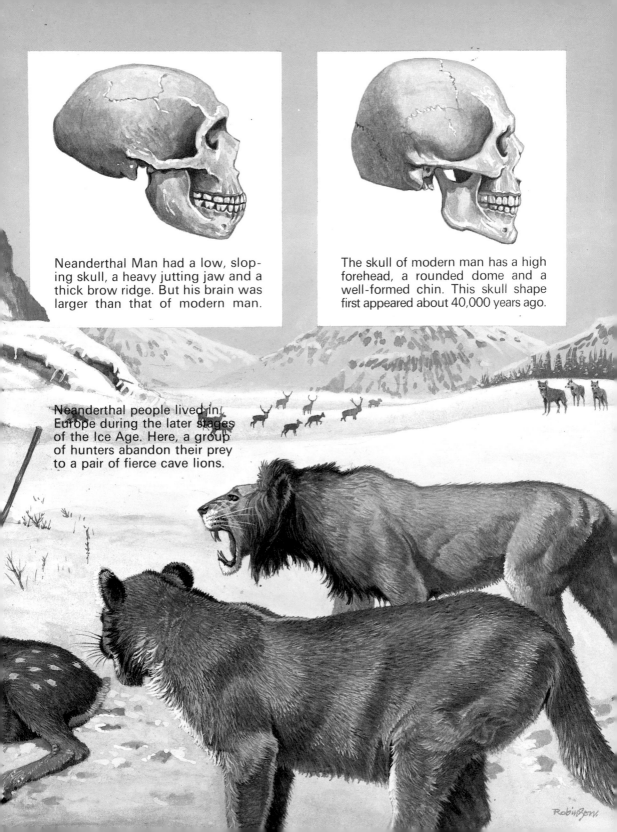

Neanderthal Man had a low, sloping skull, a heavy jutting jaw and a thick brow ridge. But his brain was larger than that of modern man.

The skull of modern man has a high forehead, a rounded dome and a well-formed chin. This skull shape first appeared about 40,000 years ago.

Neanderthal people lived in Europe during the later stages of the Ice Age. Here, a group of hunters abandon their prey to a pair of fierce cave lions.

returned. In their wake came the hunters. They sheltered in caves. To keep warm they sewed clothes from animal skins, using needles of bone and thread of sinew or wool.

Travelling bands of hunters ranged far and wide. In north-eastern Asia about 28,000 years ago, they took advantage of the retreating ice, and crossed into Alaska by a bridge of dry land. When thawing glaciers raised the levels of the sea, they became cut off from Asia by the Bering Strait.

In a similar way, human beings also made their way to Australia. For part of the way they could cross the land, but the rest was blocked by channels of water. These they crossed on rafts and in boats. In Australia they took up a life of hunting, fishing and gathering. Their way of life stayed almost unchanged until, almost 30,000 years later, 18th century Europeans came across them.

Early Villages

Groups of people that lived near rivers and lakes took to fishing with hooks, lines and nets. They also began to use simple canoes and boats. As fishermen grew more skilled their boats became

A scene of daily life among the Cro-Magnon hunters of western Europe.

larger and they ventured further afield. Big boats needed sheltered ports, and places where they could be drawn out of the water for repairs. Around such places as these, permanent settlements and villages grew up.

Farming Villages

About 10,000 years ago, people in the Middle East discovered that the grains they collected and ate were also the seeds from which new plants grew. They began to sow wild wheat and barley, and to harvest the grain when it was ripe.

Looking after the fields did not allow people to hunt very far. Instead, they captured animals and kept them to milk and breed. Sheep and goats were the first beasts to be domesticated. Later, cattle, pigs and chickens were also kept. Wherever people started to farm, permanent settlements arose that rapidly grew into villages and towns.

Middle Eastern farmers were able to grow more grain and breed more animals than they needed for themselves. They could trade their surplus for other things, while some people were able to give up farming to practice other skills. Builders made homes out of sunbaked mud bricks, and were paid for their work in grain and animals. Spinners and weavers made woollen blankets and clothing, while potters turned out baked clay pots. Soon thriving villages developed, where people made their living from many different kinds of jobs.

One of the oldest towns in the Middle East was Jericho, where people settled because of the good supply of water and salt. Another town, Catal Hüyük, grew up near a source of volcanic rock called *obsidian*. This rock was very useful because it could easily be worked into sharp tools such as axes.

The First Cities

The earliest villages lay mainly in rolling, wooded country where there was plenty of rain. But it was in the great river valleys of the Nile, Tigris and Euphrates in the Middle East, the Indus in India and the Hwang-ho in China, that the first cities arose.

Though rainfall was infrequent there, water was plentiful and could be brought to the fields by a network of ditches. Also, the rivers flooded frequently and left thick layers of silt on the fields when they receded. This rich earth was highly fertile. It meant that crops could be grown in the same fields year after year.

Sumer Time

Six thousand years ago, the Tigris and Euphrates rivers still flowed to the sea separately. They embraced a region of swamp, marsh and low plain known as Sumer. Here, over the years, clusters of villages created a huge irrigation network. Hundreds of dams, canals and ditches controlled the rivers' floodwaters and brought water to the fields.

It took many people to run this irrigation system and to control the planting and harvesting of the crops. At some point between 4000 and 3500 BC the Sumerians solved this problem by creating large centres of administration. They built storehouses around their temples. Builders, craftsmen and merchants also lived and worked here. For the first time in history people had made the big leap from villages to cities.

As cities such as Eridu, Lagash and Ur became richer, a very elaborate way of life grew up. At the centre of these cities were the temples, where local gods were worshipped by priests. In and around the temples were storehouses for surplus grain. Draught animals, such as oxen and donkeys, were kept here too. Temple officials kept records of the stores, and controlled the times of planting and harvesting. An army of architects, clothmakers, cooks, goldsmiths, musicians, traders and workers lived nearby.

In time, the land of Sumer became a patchwork of city-states. Each one was built around its temple and was surrounded by a region of irrigated farmland that supplied it with food.

As the cities grew richer they began to trade far and wide. Merchant ships ranged around the Arabian Gulf, while merchants on foot travelled north for metals, wood and wheeled vehicles.

Between 2800 and 2400 BC the cities of Sumer reached their height. They jostled for power and wealth, and they fought regularly with each other. At different times, one or another city would triumph and dominate its neighbours. But the riches of Sumer were a powerful magnet to other people too. Around 2400 BC, the Akkadians to the north grew very powerful. Led by their ruler, Sargon, they attacked and conquered Sumer. The empire of the Akkadians became the first to rule the whole of Mesopotamia – the region between the Arabian Gulf and the eastern Mediterranean.

Thousands of free men, not slaves, worked to build the great pyramids of ancient Egypt.

The Rise of Egypt

Some centuries after the rise of the Sumerian city-states, a great civilization sprang up in the narrow valley of the Nile river in Egypt. Here, flanked on both sides by arid desert and to the north protected by the sea, dozens of bustling villages and towns grew up.

Over the years the Egyptians built a vast system of dams and canals to deal with the yearly floods of the Nile, and to bring water to their crops. The river also served as the main highway of the area. It was the only reliable link between the towns that dotted the riverbanks for hundreds of kilometres. Regular winds guided the boats up river. Rowers, helped by the current, brought them downstream again.

Around 3100 BC a strong king, named Menes, united all of Egypt for the first time under his rule. In the centuries that followed, the kings (or pharaohs as they were called) became extremely powerful. Under their leadership Egyptian civilization flourished in splendour for almost 2000 years.

The ancient Egyptians believed that their pharaohs were half-gods. Pharaohs were also very rich, since they owned all the land. Anyone who farmed had to give the pharaoh part of the harvest as tax. This tribute paid for the court and its officials, for the army, and for the splendid buildings and monuments that the pharaohs built.

Some of the most spectacular structures built by the Egyptians were the tombs of dead pharaohs. Early in their history these were flat-topped. But after about 2700 BC, the style changed to a pyramid shape. It took an army of architects, stonemasons and workers to cut the stone blocks, ferry them along the Nile, and then drag them to the site in the desert. There they were assembled into a pyramid.

Inside, the dead pharaoh was laid to rest in a tomb. The treasures he owned during his life were laid out around him. One reason why we know so much about everyday Egyptian life is that many of these objects – scrolls, beds, furniture, baskets, glassware, sand clocks, gems and precious jewellery – have survived the centuries inside these tombs more or less intact.

Greek hoplite wearing Corinthian helmet

THE SPREAD OF CIVILIZATION

As the power and influence of Egypt and Mesopotamia grew, it hastened the spread of civilization throughout the Middle East. Trade, by land and by sea, brought distant people into contact with these great empires. Sailors ventured to and fro across the Mediterranean, and along its coasts as far west as the Atlantic.

In the Aegean an entire civilization arose that was based on trade. The ships of the Minoans of Crete sailed between their island home and Egypt and Greece, carrying wheat, oil, copper and pottery. But about 1450 BC, the Minoans vanished mysteriously from history. To this day nobody is certain why. Some people think that they were wiped out by earthquakes, after a huge volcanic explosion on the nearby island of Thera.

Turmoil in the Middle East

Around 1200 BC, the entire world of the eastern Mediterranean was plunged into a period of turmoil and upheaval. Waves of roving pirate bands and fierce barbarians swept through the area. Empire followed empire. First the Hittites, then the Assyrians, the Chaldeans and others sprang to power and fell again before the next wave of

Mycenaean bronze helmet around 1000 BC

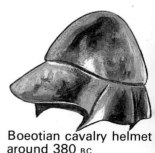

Boeotian cavalry helmet around 380 BC

conquerors. Each group of invaders introduced new and better weapons of war with which they crushed their foe. First came battle chariots, then siege engines and warships. Later, came steel weapons and horse cavalry.

The Rise of Ancient Greece

At various times the peninsula of Greece was overrun by barbarian tribes. These swept out of the north and eventually reached the islands of the Aegean and the coast of western Anatolia (modern Turkey). They established many small kingdoms. But the land was mountainous and there was not nearly enough farmland for all. As these kingdoms grew, they turned more and more to the sea and to trade.

By 700 BC, several Greek states had become quite powerful and wealthy. They began to establish colonies for their surplus population. Soon, they were flourishing along the length and breadth of the Mediterranean and Black Seas.

As the city-states expanded they began to clash sharply with the powerful empire of the Persians. Under Cyrus the Great (559–530 BC), Persia had grown to include the entire Middle East, from Egypt and Anatolia to north-eastern India. Friction between the Greeks and the Persians flared into a series of wars early in the 5th century BC. Led by Darius and then

Roman legionary

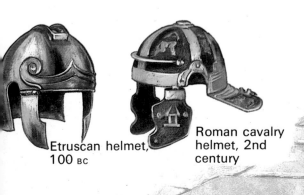

Etruscan helmet, 100 BC

Roman cavalry helmet, 2nd century

Xerxes, the Persians invaded Greece twice. They were forced to withdraw both times, by smaller Greek armies who fought fiercely to defend their home.

There then followed a period during which Greek civilization flowered in a way that few have before or since. In what became known as the 'Golden Age' the arts and sciences flourished, and the influence of the Greeks left its mark on the whole Mediterranean world.

Almost inevitably, however, differences arose between the many city-states. A long war broke out between Athens and Sparta, and their allies, that sapped the strength of the Greeks and led to their downfall. Powerful outsiders led by Philip of Macedon easily defeated the Greek cities and united the country under Macedonian rule.

Alexander the Great, Philip's son, went on to become one of the greatest generals the world has ever seen. He led a large army of Greeks and Macedonians into Asia, and in 11 years defeated the mighty Persian Empire. He got as far as India with his troops. He died in 323 BC, at the young age of 33 years; perhaps from poison. Within a few years his vast empire came apart at the seams, as his generals quarrelled and divided up his conquests.

The Roman Empire

While the empire of Alexander the Great fell apart in the east, a new power was growing in the western Mediterranean that was soon to control the entire ancient world from Europe to Asia.

By 265 BC the Romans had expanded from their original base in central Italy, to control the whole peninsula. Soon after that they challenged the might of Carthage, then the greatest sea power in the western Mediterranean. By 241 BC, the Romans had driven the Carthaginians out of Sicily. This island became the first of Rome's many overseas provinces.

Led by their brilliant general, Hannibal, the Carthaginians struck back. They marched from North Africa through Spain and France, and crossed the Alps into Italy itself. For 12 years the two armies struggled until the Carthaginians fell, exhausted, back to North Africa. Now it was the Romans' turn to attack their enemy's home base. In 146 BC, almost 100 years after they first clashed with Carthage, the Romans destroyed the city and razed it to the ground.

In the following century Roman soldiers swept through Greece, Anatolia and Syria. Under the command of Julius Caesar they took Gaul and all of Europe

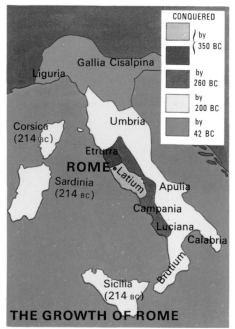

CONQUERED

	by 350 BC
	by 260 BC
	by 200 BC
	by 42 BC

Gallia Cisalpina
Liguria
Corsica (214 BC)
Umbria
Etruria
ROME · Latium
Sardinia (214 BC)
Apulia
Campania
Luciana
Calabria
Bruttium
Sicilia (214 BC)

THE GROWTH OF ROME

The growth of Rome as a kingdom and as a republic between 350 BC and 42 BC.

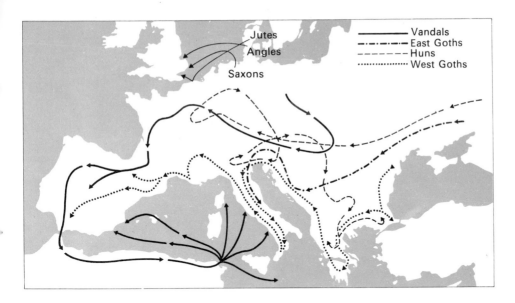

Barbarian invaders swept into Europe out of the great plains of Central Asia after the collapse of the Roman Empire.

west of the Rhine. Some years later, Britain was conquered too.

In 30 BC, Rome officially ceased to be a republic. The dictator Octavian set himself up as emperor. He took the title of Augustus Caesar. By the reign of the emperor Trajan, in AD 117, the Roman Empire reached its greatest size ever. It stretched from the Atlantic Ocean in the west, through Europe and North Africa as far east as Mesopotamia and Persia. The city of Rome itself grew until it had a population of over a million people.

Rome's great strength was its ability to govern this vast empire in an orderly way, and also to hold dozens of nations and tribes together in a single unit. The Romans achieved this by dividing the empire into provinces. Each province was ruled by a paid governor. But even with a huge professional army to support them, the Romans knew that they could never govern effectively without the loyalty of the local people too. For this reason, the Romans allowed their conquered subjects to follow their own customs and traditions. To a large extent they were even allowed to rule themselves. In return, many subjects were honoured by being made citizens of Rome. The provinces also received all the benefits of years of peace and order, and of the empire's enormous wealth.

The Fall of Rome
In time, however, the empire proved simply too big and too unwieldy to run. Political power struggles, the economic decline of Italy, the cost of the huge professional army and the growing pressure of barbarian attacks all took their toll. In AD 286 the emperor Diocletian tried to make the empire easier to rule and defend. He split it in two, and set up an emperor of the west in Rome while he himself took control of the east. A century later, Constantine the Great established the eastern capital at Constantinople – the city was renamed after him.

But the barbarian invasions and the general decline could not be halted. In AD 476, the western empire collapsed when Rome was sacked and burned by invaders. But the eastern empire, propped up by its huge wealth and military strength, continued to thrive for centuries until it was finally overwhelmed by Moslem armies.

The Barbarian Invasions

With the collapse of the Roman Empire in the west, waves of barbarian tribes swept across Europe. They came from the plains of central Asia, from Russia, northern Europe and Scandinavia. Peoples such as the Huns, Goths and Vandals spilled into the former Roman provinces, that today are Britain, France, Spain and North Africa. They also invaded Italy.

At first these warlike tribes mainly raided and looted rich villas and towns. Later they began to settle and defend their newly-won lands. Small kingdoms arose, each with its own laws and customs. But although the old Roman ways of life vanished, some traditions still survived. The Church remained the centre of religious life and of learning, and Latin was still the universal language of Europe. As the barbarian tribes rapidly converted to Christianity a common link was forged between them and their neighbours.

Though the term 'barbarian' was used by the Romans to describe people who lived outside the empire, it did not mean that they were primitive savages. They were highly skilled in making tools and weapons, and produced some of the most magnificent metalwork ever seen. They were famous for the beautiful gold and

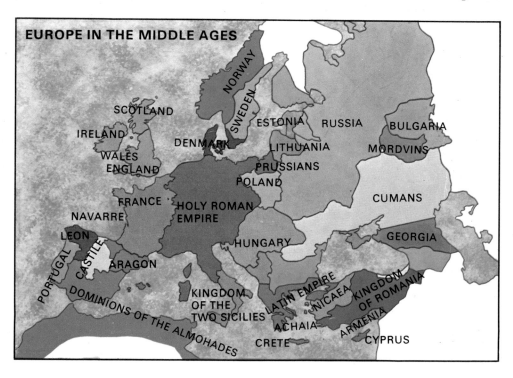

EUROPE IN THE MIDDLE AGES

silver brooches and clasps they wore. These were often inlaid with precious stones and bore delicate designs.

Barbarian Settlements

Many barbarian tribes settled in small farming villages. They kept herds of cattle and sometimes sheep and goats. Pigs were let loose to forage in nearby woods. Surrounding their villages were pastures and tilled fields where crops such as wheat, barley, rye and beans were raised.

KEY TO PARTS OF ARMOUR

1. visor   6. greave
2. breastplate   7. sabaton
3. gauntlet
4. couter
5. cuisse

Plate armour, about 1500

Norman

Saracen

Crusader

13th Century helmet

THE MIDDLE AGES

Slowly, life in Europe settled into a regular pattern that came to be known as the feudal system. It grew out of the practice of kings and powerful lords granting their loyal followers areas of land. In return, the followers promised to serve them in times of war.

The feudal system began in the 800s among the Franks of France. From there it spread rapidly throughout the rest of western Europe.

The person at the top of the feudal system was the king. He granted land to his barons who, in turn, handed out estates to minor nobles and knights. These gave parcels of land to the serfs, who farmed it. Serfs could be freemen, who worked their own small fields and paid over part of the harvest as rent. Many serfs, however, were almost slaves.

The feudal system centred about the manors or castles of the lords. In the event of attack they provided their people with shelter in their forts. If the lord went off to battle, his followers went with him.

Forts and Castles

The heart of every feudal estate was the fortified home of the lord. Early forts were just crude mounds of earth, ringed by wooden fences. As lords became wealthier and more powerful, they built large castles of stone surrounded by wide moats to keep attackers at bay. The walls were high to shield those inside from arrows and missiles, and thick enough to withstand battering rams and rocks hurled by catapults.

Inside the walls there were wells, stalls for the livestock, living quarters for soldiers, and workshops and homes for the castle defenders.

In the Middle Ages there were no police or armies to keep the peace. But since bandits and raiders were a constant threat, every estate was a fort.

1. Early castles were simple wooden towers, fenced in.

2. Knights later built stronger castles with a strong central tower or keep.

3. Castles grew in size, and became much more complicated in layout.

4. Castles built on rocky hills were especially hard to attack.

5. Some had deep ditches and water-filled moats around them.

146

The Black Death

During the mid 1300s a catastrophe struck Europe, that wiped out one person in four. The terrible epidemic of bubonic plague, which became known as the Black Death, swept from the Middle East to Ireland in the space of five years. Unknown to people of the time, the plague was spread by rats. It killed about 25 million people. The effect was terrible. Entire villages and towns were wiped out. One far-reaching effect was that the feudal system was weakened. Everywhere farms were abandoned, and the land fell into neglect.

The Hundred Years War

The Middle Ages was a restless and

violent time. Nowhere is this better shown than by the drawn-out struggle between France and England, that became known as the Hundred Years War. Between 1337 and 1453, these two nations fought a long series of wars over the English claim to the throne of France. After endless battles at sea and on land, the English were finally driven out of France. Only the town of Calais was left in their possession.

The Crusades

Christianity was the main focus of everyday life in the Middle Ages. The influence of the Church was felt by everyone from kings to serfs. Its wealth and power can be seen by the many

Life in the late Middle Ages was luxurious for the lucky few who were rich and powerful. But for most people life was hard and cruel.

splendid churches, cathedrals and palaces that still stand in Europe today.

The capture of Palestine and Jerusalem by Moslem armies was a great shock to Christian Europe. The harassing of pilgrims strengthened their anger. Pope Urban II called for a holy crusade, to drive the 'infidel' armies out of the Holy Land. Between 1096 and 1270, eight crusades set off from Europe. Their effect was tremendous. Europeans got a taste of eastern luxury, and many new ideas in medicine, science and learning were introduced. Trade grew when nobles sought out spices, wines and fine clothes from the East.

The Close of the Middle Ages

If any one event could be said to mark the end of the Middle Ages it would be the fall of Constantinople, the capital of the Byzantine Empire. In 1453, after a 54-day siege, this great city on the eastern fringe of Europe was overwhelmed by an army of 150,000 Turks. With it ended an empire that had flourished since Roman times. From now on the centre of western civilization would shift westward – first to Italy, and then north over the Alps to the rest of Europe.

The Renaissance

The word 'Renaissance' is French for 'rebirth'. It is the name given to the period in which the Middle Ages ended and the modern world began. It started in Italy during the 1400s, and reached its height in the rest of Europe over the next 200 years.

The Renaissance was marked by an outburst of interest in art, science and all other forms of learning. It began with the rediscovery of knowledge from ancient Greece and Rome, and soon branched out in other directions too. During this time travel and exploration flourished, trade increased, and cities sprang up and grew rich.

The Art of Printing

One of the biggest encouragements to the spread of learning was the growth of printing. In 1454, a German printer called Gutenberg began using moveable pieces of metal type. He cast each letter from a standard mould, and then set them into words and sentences. He arranged these in a flat tray to make up a single page. His press could print up to 300 such pages in a single day.

As the art of printing spread, it became

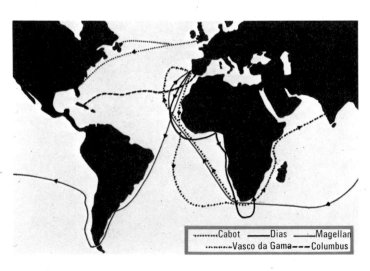

The routes of the explorers Cabot, Dias, Magellan, da Gama and Columbus show how they fanned out from Europe, searching for new trade routes to the East.

........Cabot ———Dias ——Magellan
......Vasco da Gama———Columbus

possible to produce many more copies of books than ever before. They could now reach a much wider public. In this way, new ideas were spread far and wide throughout Europe.

The Role of the Church
In the Middle Ages, the Christian Church was the centre of learning in Europe. Its influence was seen in all areas of knowledge. But with the rise of independent universities, such as those at Bologna in Italy, and Paris in France, learning spread to people who were not directly part of the Church.

This was a time when people were fascinated with the thinkers of the ancient world. It led them to question many of the existing beliefs in art, science, religion and politics. The influence of the Romans and Greeks, for example, led painters and sculptors to present very accurate and realistic human figures for the first time. In a similar way new styles of architecture arose, and scientists began to study the laws of nature. Inventors experimented in every area.

The Reformation
One major outcome of the Renaissance was that people began to question the beliefs of the Church. They also became more critical of its great wealth and power, and of the way in which the Church was run.

In 1517 a German monk, named Martin Luther, protested against many of the Church's worst practices. He found a ready audience. Support for his complaints, and those of others, swelled rapidly in Germany, Switzerland, Scandinavia and Britain. When this rebellion finally broke away from the Church of Rome, it took the name Protestantism – the religion of the protestors.

The Church replied by bringing in many new reforms over the following years. Eventually, this entire period of protest and reform became known as the Reformation.

The Age of Discovery
The Renaissance is notable for being the era in which Europeans ranged far and wide, exploring the world as never before. Some voyages of discovery were made purely out of curiosity. But most were attempts to open up trade routes and conquer new lands.

The greatest voyages were not overland, but by sea. These became possible as ships became larger, with higher decks and stronger rudders and rigging. They could ride out the rough weather of the Atlantic and Indian Oceans. As compasses and sextants improved, it was also possible to steer across open ocean, instead of staying close to shore.

The earliest trips were made to discover a route to the East, and to break the Arab hold on the spice and silk trade. The Portugese, encouraged by their ruler Prince Henry the Navigator, led the way. They explored the route around Africa. By 1499 their first ships reached India, and soon started a regular trade in pepper and spices.

A few years earlier, in 1492, Christopher Columbus took a small fleet of Spanish ships across the Atlantic. He hoped to find a western route to India. Columbus found a chain of islands that were part of America, at that stage undiscovered. But Columbus never recognized his mistake. He died some years later, still thinking he had found the western route to India, even though other explorers had found he was wrong.

The first European to sail around the world was a Portugese navigator named Magellan. His fleet of five Spanish ships left Europe in 1519. Three years later the one surviving ship and its exhausted crew returned to Spain, having circled the globe. Magellan himself was killed in a fight with natives of the Philippines. In the meantime, other Portugese were sailing still further east. In 1513 they reached China, and in 1545, a Portugese ship arrived at Japan.

The Rise of Europe
During the 1600s and 1700s the nations of Europe grew tremendously in power. Between them they came to dominate much of the world.

In North America, the English and French founded colonies along the eastern coast. Some of the earliest settlers to arrive were a boatload of Puritans who fled from England to find religious freedom. In 1620 their ship, the *Mayflower*, landed in the bay of Cape Cod. They were the forerunners of the colonists who, 155 years later, were to break away from England and form the United States of America.

South America was settled by the Spanish and Portugese. In the 1500s they wiped out the great civilizations of the Incas and the Mayas, and established thriving colonies, that grew rich from mining silver, and from farming.

Trade with the East
In Africa the first settlements grew up along the sailing routes to the East, wherever ships put in for supplies and repairs. The Dutch settled around the Cape of Good Hope, and the French in Madagascar. Meanwhile, trade with India and the Far East grew and became highly profitable. The East India companies of England, Holland and France made a fortune through their control of this trade. The Dutch company ruled the region now known as Indonesia, while the French and English struggled for the mastery of India. By 1757 the English had won, and had established their rule over most of that country.

Slowly a pattern emerged that was to be repeated again and again. Once a regular trade was established, European nations protected their interests by bringing in troops, and building harbours and forts. Settlers soon followed, and a permanent outpost or colony grew up.

The Power of Kings
Within Europe, the role of kings reached its peak in the 1600s and 1700s. As their power grew they became able to tax their subjects as heavily as they wished. They could raise armies and fight wars when they wanted to do so. In most countries there were few, if any, limits to their power.

In France, the absolute power of the king was greatest during the reign of Louis XIV. He came to the throne in 1643, and ruled for the next 72 years without a constitution or a parliament. His will was law. But the splendid court he kept at Versailles, and the series of costly and ineffective wars he fought, left the French people poor and restless by the time he died.

In England, on the other hand, the uncontrolled power of the king was stopped by a civil war in the 1640s. King Charles I was defeated by the armies of parliament, and he was executed. Although the monarchy was restored in 1660, its powers from then on were limited and shared with ministers, and with parliament.

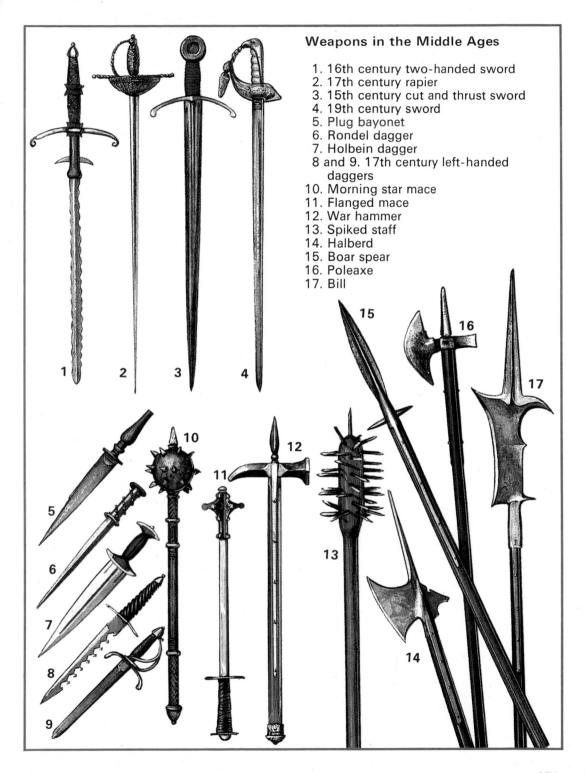

Weapons in the Middle Ages

1. 16th century two-handed sword
2. 17th century rapier
3. 15th century cut and thrust sword
4. 19th century sword
5. Plug bayonet
6. Rondel dagger
7. Holbein dagger
8 and 9. 17th century left-handed daggers
10. Morning star mace
11. Flanged mace
12. War hammer
13. Spiked staff
14. Halberd
15. Boar spear
16. Poleaxe
17. Bill

The Thirty Years War

In 1618 a devastating religious struggle broke out in Europe. The Thirty Years War began as a local struggle between Protestant and Catholic princes in Germany. But the fighting soon spread to include France, Spain, Austria, Sweden and Denmark. The war dragged on for years without conclusion. By the time a peace was reached in 1648, much of Germany had been devastated and millions of people had died.

Two Revolutions

The close of the 1700s saw two kinds of revolution breaking out in Europe. One kind was political, violent and bloody. The second was industrial, and changed the face of Europe as few would ever have imagined.

The War of Independence

The first of the political revolutions to break out took place in North America. The 13 English colonies there rebelled, saying that British rule was tyrannical and undemocratic. They claimed that it served only British interests, not those of the colonies, and that it did not permit the colonists to have any real say in their own affairs.

The American War of Independence lasted from 1775 to 1783. At first the British troops seemed to be winning. But a series of defeats at the hands of the American army, led by George Washington, led to British surrender in 1781. Two years later a peace treaty was signed, recognizing the United States as an independent country.

The French Revolution

The second great political revolution took place in France. It erupted in 1789, toppling the family of kings that had ruled the country for years and sending shockwaves throughout Europe.

France was plunged in crisis at the time the revolution broke out. The country was deep in debt, and the government was badly run. In a desperate effort to raise new taxes, King Louis XVI summoned the national parliament – the *Estates General*. But his efforts to control it failed and he was forced to back down. He tried to flee the country in 1792, to get support from Austria and Prussia. However, he was captured and imprisoned. The monarchy was soon abolished and Louis was executed.

The revolution went through a period of violence and terror, as various groups struggled for control. In the end, power passed to a young army officer whose genius in battle made him look like France's saviour. His name was Napoleon Bonaparte.

At first he seemed unbeatable, and by 1804 he had taken the title of Emperor. Over the next ten years he fought almost every nation in Europe. By 1812 his successes had given France control of much of the continent. But in the end Napoleon overreached himself. He was defeated and exiled, and died in St Helena in the south Atlantic in 1821.

In the end, the French Revolution fell victim to its own ideals – those of 'Liberty, Equality and Fraternity'. But its impact was immense. During the 1800s it survived as an inspiration to countless movements of national independence.

Right: Guns developed swiftly after the early years of the Renaissance. Heavy siege cannon became lighter, so they could be moved rapidly and positioned for use during battle. Handguns such as rifles and muskets became standard weapons, too.

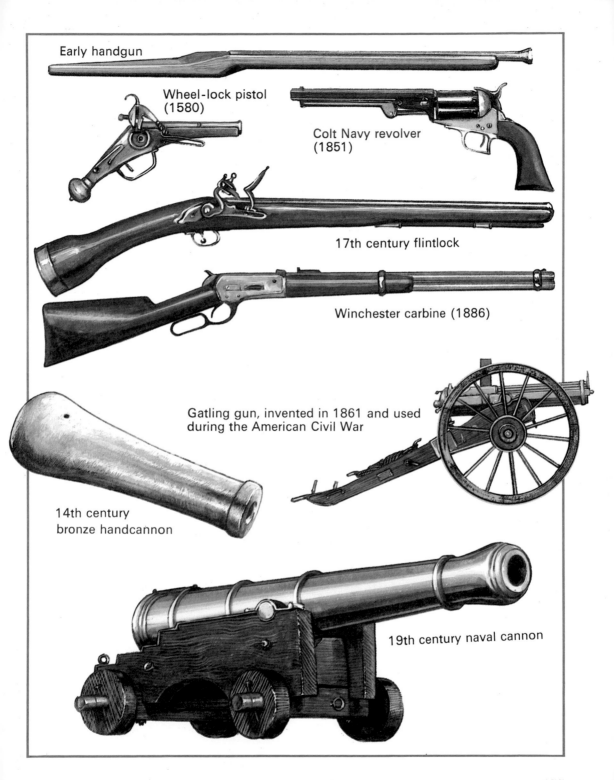

Early handgun

Wheel-lock pistol
(1580)

Colt Navy revolver
(1851)

17th century flintlock

Winchester carbine (1886)

Gatling gun, invented in 1861 and used
during the American Civil War

14th century
bronze handcannon

19th century naval cannon

Uniforms Through the Ages

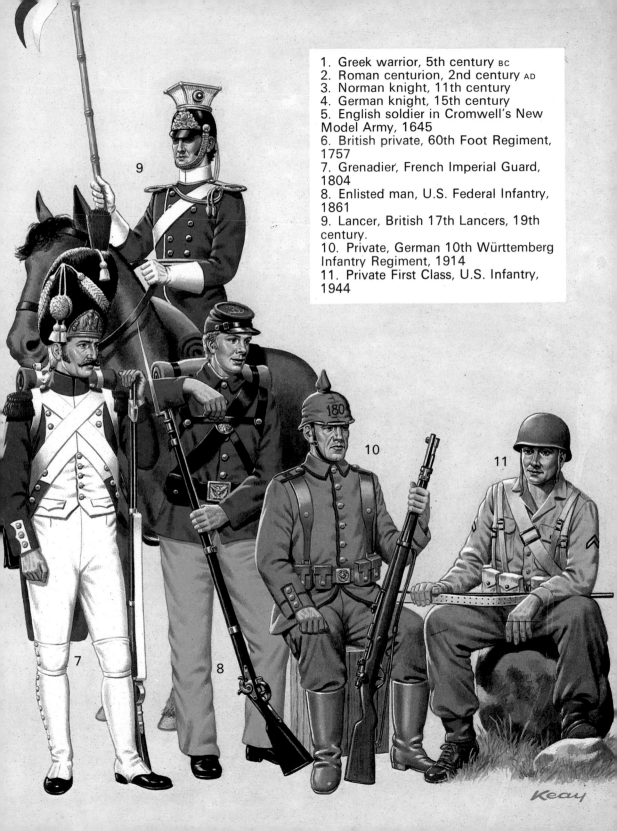

1. Greek warrior, 5th century BC
2. Roman centurion, 2nd century AD
3. Norman knight, 11th century
4. German knight, 15th century
5. English soldier in Cromwell's New Model Army, 1645
6. British private, 60th Foot Regiment, 1757
7. Grenadier, French Imperial Guard, 1804
8. Enlisted man, U.S. Federal Infantry, 1861
9. Lancer, British 17th Lancers, 19th century.
10. Private, German 10th Württemberg Infantry Regiment, 1914
11. Private First Class, U.S. Infantry, 1944

Keay

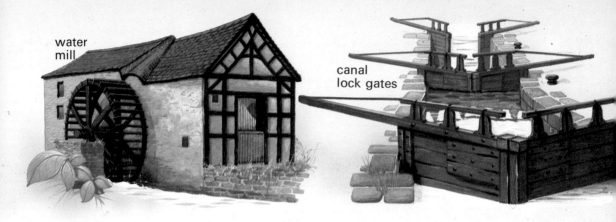

water mill

canal lock gates

The Industrial Revolution

The term 'Industrial Revolution' was invented in France in the 1830s. It described the great upheaval that was taking place in Europe and America at the time. During the 1800s, the western world was changed in ways that few people would ever have imagined. Daily life, which had been based on farming for thousands of years, now shifted to crowded cities.

The transformation worked by the Industrial Revolution did not affect everyone at once. In Britain the effects became noticeable by the mid-1700s. In Russia they only began to be widely felt 100 years after that.

Machines Make the Difference

The introduction of weaving and spinning machines in Britain was one of the first examples of the change that machines brought about. They wiped out a tradition of craftsmen making textiles at home – a tradition that had not changed for centuries – in a few dozen years. A single machine could do the work of many workers, and do it very cheaply. It became possible to ship raw cotton from India to England, turn it into cloth, and ship it all the way back to sell for less than it would have cost to make the cloth in India.

The First Factories

The earliest weaving and spinning machines were powered by waterwheels. But in 1769 an invention appeared that was to change this entirely. In that year, James Watt developed the first efficient steam engine. It could run anything from a pump or factory machine, to a train or ship. When steam engines were linked up to weaving machines, they provided power that was available day and night.

The size of steam engines made it necessary to group them and the machines in large workshops. By 1800, these had become the world's first factories. Workers flooded in every day

coal mining

railway bridge

wind mill

air balloon

by the thousands, to tend the noisy and dirty machines.

The Changing Landscape

Factory machines needed a good supply of fuel and water to keep running. New factories were often set up near sources of coal and plentiful water. Towns grew up around them, where the workers lived. As people flocked from the countryside looking for work, they too settled near the factories. Soon villages became towns, and towns grew into huge cities. The cities expanded so quickly that conditions became unbearably grim. People were crowded into dark, dirty homes, which lacked sewage, running water and electricity. Nevertheless, the population of Europe still grew at a tremendous rate. It rose from 185 million in 1800, to more than 400 million a century later. On top of this, another 60 million people left the continent to emmigrate to America, Australia and other countries.

During the Industrial Revolution, water-wheels and windmills were replaced by noisy but far more efficient steam engines. They needed enormous amounts of fuel. Coal mining grew rapidly to meet this demand. Canals and bridges were built by the hundreds, to link factories with cities and ports.

coal-fired foundry

coal mining machinery

The Revolution in Transport

Before the invention of steam transport, people mostly travelled by sail, by horse and cart, and by foot. On land the going was slow and the roads very rough. A day's journey of 35 kilometres was thought to be good going. At sea, a trip of weeks could easily drag on for months if the winds and tides were difficult.

All this changed once steam engines were harnessed for transport. In 1829, George Stephenson built a locomotive that astonished the world by reaching 46 km/h. In 1830, a regular service took passengers from Liverpool to Manchester. That year alone, 70,000 people made the 48-kilometre trip which, when nothing went wrong with the highly unreliable engines, took less than two hours.

In the years that followed, an enormous railway building boom occured. By 1836 there were almost 800 kilometres of track in Britain, and over 2000 kilometres in the United States.

Steam at Sea

Early steam engines were large and heavy, so it was far easier to fit them into boats than any kind of land vehicle. Steam-powered ships first came into use at the beginning of the 1800s. Most were paddle-wheelers, which ran best in rivers and sheltered waters. They had trouble coping with the waves of the open sea.

One of the earliest successes was

Robert Fulton's ship *Clermont*. His paddle-wheeler was put into service on the Hudson River in America. It ran between New York and Albany from 1807, and completed the 240 kilometres in just 32 hours.

Once propellers had replaced paddle wheels, steamships rapidly overtook sailing ships in size and speed. By 1850 they had become longer and heavier than any sail-powered rivals. They were also able to cross the Atlantic on regular schedules, something no sailing ship could ever hope to match. Voyages that had once taken at least a month or more were cut down to days. By 1900 the fastest ships crossed in a week, and arrived at their destinations almost to the hour.

THE AGE OF EMPIRES

From the middle of the 1800s until World War I erupted in 1914, the nations of Europe left their mark on almost every part of the world. In the short space of 50 years they set up colonies, and overran much of Asia and America, and almost all of Africa. Never before or since was Europe able to dominate the world so completely. The effects of this time can still be seen today.

Imperial Powers
All the empires that were established were built on Europe's extraordinary military might, and the great wealth

Main railway stations in the 1800s grew to be huge iron and glass structures.

created by its thriving industries. Europe's factories were turning out ships, railways, bridges and similar goods that were the best in the world. They were shipped everywhere. In return, the colonies that were founded supplied their parent countries with raw materials of every description. A pattern emerged, and wherever European explorers, traders and soldiers went they established control and swiftly carved out new territories to add to their empires.

The greatest imperial power of all was Britain. It acquired colonies in so many parts of the globe, it could boast that the Sun never set on its far-flung possessions. France was not far behind, and Holland, Germany, Belgium, Spain, Portugal and Italy all had colonies too.

In Asia, the Dutch controlled the islands of Indonesia. The French had Indochina, and the British dominated Malaya and the great sub-continent of India. In China, almost every European nation, including Russia, had interests. The Japanese and Americans appeared on the scene too. They competed for bases and special trading rights, on terms that were so one-sided that the Chinese almost lost control of their own country.

The Scramble for Africa

In the early years of the 1800s, most of Africa was a mystery to Europeans. Only the fringes of the continent had been explored. Along the coasts there were a few bases that served as fueling stations for ships on the way to the East, and as trading depots with the interior. They dealt mostly in slaves, ivory and timber.

All this was to change after the great voyages of discovery. These began in the 1860s, and soon opened up the heart of Africa. What followed was a frantic scramble by European countries to control every inch of the continent. With the British firmly established in the south, and the French in the north and west, what remained was carved up by Belgium, Germany, Portugal, Spain and Italy. By 1902, the only two independent countries in all Africa were Liberia and Ethiopia.

The early years of the 1900s mark the high point of European power and influence. A few years later, all of Europe was plunged into a conflict so bitter and violent that its whole way of life was changed forever.

World War I

World War I, some people argue, was a war begun by accident. The event that triggered it off was the shooting of an Austrian archduke, Franz Ferdinand, in Sarejevo, a town in Serbia.

That such an out-of-the-way incident could plunge all of Europe into war seems incredible. But at the time an extraordinary rivalry existed in almost every area of national power and prestige. The major nations of Europe were all linked by a series of alliances, committing them to support one another if fighting ever broke out. Germany and the Austro-Hungarian empire were on one side, with Russia, Britain and France on the other.

Both sides had detailed and very complex plans for getting their troops into battle. It was a slow process, however, and if one nation started to move their troops it was a clear signal to the others that they should start too.

Russia, whose armies had furthest to travel, began to mobilize its troops soon after Austria attacked Serbia. In rapid succession Germany, France and Britain became caught up in the process as well.

162

Later on, the two sides were also joined by Turkey and Bulgaria. These countries fought with Germany. Japan, Italy and the United States fought with France, Britain and the Commonwealth countries.

The War in the West
In the first weeks German armies swept through Belgium and into northern France, aiming for Paris. Their drive was

The introduction of tanks helped to break the stalemate of trench warfare. They could easily cross trenches and smash holes in lines of defence.

British fighters attack German tanks during a desert battle in North Africa, in World War II.

halted at the Marne river, just short of their goal. Both sides dug into defensive positions, with the Germans on one side and the British and French on the other. Soon a vast system of trenches stretched from the English Channel all the way to Switzerland. Behind this more-or-less fixed line, the two sides battered each other for four years.

Millions of soldiers were thrown into a war that had no solution. The weapons with which they were armed were so deadly that the best both sides could do was to slaughter the other's soldiers by the hundreds of thousands. Between 1914 and 1918, an almost unbelievable ten million people were killed.

The War in the East

The war in the East was never such a stalemate as in the West. Russia at first made some gains, but its poorly equipped armies were no match for Germany. Russian losses were astronomical, and soon exhausted the country's ability to continue the fight. After the revolution of November 1917, the new Soviet government that had overthrown the Tsar signed a peace treaty with the Germans.

The war ended as the German defences in the West began to crumble, and the exhausted country neared collapse. In the peace treaties that were signed in 1919, Germany lost all its overseas territories and much of its land in eastern Europe. Germany was also made to pay an enormous sum of money, as compensation for the wreckage caused by the war.

The Inter-War Years

The years between 1918 and 1939 were anything but peaceful. In Germany there was a lot of political unrest. It led to the rise of Adolf Hitler and the Nazi Party, who had sworn to change the outcome of the war that had so recently ended. Hitler built up a huge army and airforce, and turned Germany into a powerful military nation again.

Elsewhere, the world was plunged into upheaval by the Great Depression of the 1930s. Millions lost their jobs and all their savings. In 1931, in America alone, 12 million people were without work. Not until the end of the decade did business once more start to return to normal. By then, the world had been drawn into another war.

World War II

In September 1939, Germany invaded and overran Poland. The following spring German armies captured Denmark and Norway, and swept through Belgium, the Netherlands and France in the space of seven weeks. By 1942 Germany controlled Europe from the Atlantic to the Black Sea, and from Norway to North Africa.

In the Pacific a surprise Japanese attack crippled the US fleet at Pearl Harbor, in Hawaii. Within months the Japanese also took all of Southeast Asia, and began moving toward Australia. But the tide turned now that the United States was drawn into the fight. After 1942, US forces slowly retook the Pacific islands held by the Japanese. In August 1945, two atomic bombs were dropped on Japan, with horrifying effects. The Pacific war was over.

The war in Europe had ended a few months earlier, in May 1945, less than a year after a vast Allied invasion force stormed the beaches of Normandy. Caught between the Allied push from the west and the Russian drive from the east, Germany was finally defeated.

An anti-submarine missile drops a torpedo by parachute.

The Tornado, a modern multi-role combat aircraft.

A sea-launched Cruise missile springs from the ocean.

The After-effects

World War II was the most terrible war so far known. It is thought that more than 50 million people were killed during the struggle.

Germany was divided in two after the war, and Allied forces remain stationed there to this day. In eastern Europe the Soviet Union established its influence over East Germany, Czechoslovakia, Poland, Romania and Bulgaria. Communist governments have been set up in these countries.

Modern pilotless planes.

The Russian Scamp system, a mobile missile that can be fired from a tank.

THE MODERN WORLD

Since the end of World War II, the two leading countries of the world have been the United States and the Soviet Union. These two are often referred to as the 'superpowers'. During much of this time, the two countries have confronted each other in a state of armed truce. Each is too powerful to be attacked, yet neither is able to ignore or defeat the other.

Contests between the two have taken many forms, not all of them military, and have taken place in many parts of the world. In both the Korean War (1950–1953) and the Vietnam War (1964–1975) the superpowers were involved, even if only indirectly. Both events drew them into efforts to maintain or expand their influence in the world.

One of the most important developments since 1945 has been the disappearance of the great European

A shoulder-launched anti-aircraft missile.

RUSH

empires of the 1800s. By the end of the war, colonies everywhere were demanding their independence. Both France and Britain were either forced, or volunteered, to grant them their wish. They were followed a few years later by Spain and Portugal. Today, almost all of Africa and Asia consist of independent nations.

The United Nations

Out of the alliance of nations that formed in World War II to fight Germany and Japan, there arose a new international organization – the United Nations. It was officially founded in San Francisco in 1945, with 51 members. Today it has its headquarters in New York, and a membership of over 130 nations.

The United Nations provides a vital meeting place, where countries can exchange views and air their differences. It also runs a number of important international organizations that deal with world health, education, disaster relief and refugees. These organizations provide aid to developing countries all over the world.

The Space Race

The contest to invent and build bigger and better military weapons drew the United States and the Soviet Union into a spectacular space race. It began with the launch of a small orbiting satellite, Sputnik I, by the Soviet Union in 1957. The USA reacted with alarm, and rushed to catch up in whatever ways possible. Initially it met with numerous setbacks, and it was the Russians who first managed to put a man in space. Yuri Gagarin, their cosmonaut, was fired aloft in 1963.

In the next few years the Americans caught up quickly, with a series of impressive space flights. In 1969, they managed to land two astronauts on the surface of the Moon. Since then, they have made a number of other Moon landings. The Russians focused their efforts on building orbiting stations, where cosmonauts could live and work for months at a time. In the 1970s, a series of robot explorer satellites were fired to other planets. They have so far provided us with the first glimpse of the Universe beyond Earth.

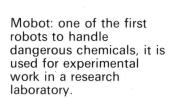

Mobot: one of the first robots to handle dangerous chemicals, it is used for experimental work in a research laboratory.

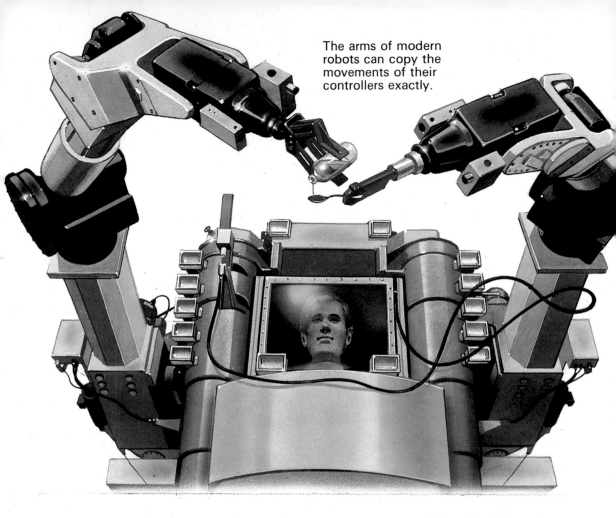

The arms of modern robots can copy the movements of their controllers exactly.

Problems in the Modern World

People in today's world face an enormous range of problems, that will have to be dealt with in the near future. However, few can agree about the best way in which they should be handled.

Some of the most likely problems to find a solution are epidemic diseases, that have always taken a high toll of human life. To fight them, massive campaigns have been mounted in many parts of the world. Polio is one disease that has been checked in this way, while smallpox is now thought to be almost wiped out. Other campaigns, such as the one against malaria, have met with setbacks that were not expected. It will still be a long time before this disease is successfully controlled.

As standards of health improve, the population of many countries has started to grow at an enormous rate. In many nations the problems of feeding, housing and educating everyone is a daunting and very expensive task indeed. Feeding the world's people is an increasingly important problem in our world. If all the world's food were equally shared out, there would be enough for everyone. But this does not happen. Almost half the world's people do not get enough to eat, and many die of starvation. New ways of farming, and organizing food distribution, will have to be found.

Another major problem of the modern world is caused by the effects of our activities on our world. Pollution, caused by waste products from industry and farming being dumped in the water supply, the sea and the air, is one of the biggest dangers we face.

The Crisis in Energy
Since 1973, the world has had to cope with soaring oil and gas prices. It has also had to face up to local shortages of all forms of energy. During this time the demand for energy has grown steadily, while many of the world's leading oil producers have raised prices and limited their output of crude oil. The rest of the world has had to find a way to pay huge fuel bills on the one hand, and to save energy and find new sources on the other. Many nations have now begun to search for forms of energy such as nuclear power and solar power, in preparation for the future.

The Future
In the years up to the end of this century, one of the greatest changes we will see will be in the way industry is run. More and more use will be made of computers and automatic processes – such as robots – to handle simple tasks, and to run assembly lines. Many people will lose their present jobs and will have to find work in tourism, travel and other leisure industries. Others will take jobs servicing and running the new machines.

In the home, many new electronically controlled devices will appear. They will simplify household chores, and leave people with free time for other kinds of work and activities.

There are no human workers in this part of an automobile factory. Instead, the work is done by robots. The automobile bodies are moved automatically along the assembly line. One-armed robot welders fix the parts of each body together.

Factory robots can be given different kinds of grippers or 'fingers'. The robot can move the gripper up and down, and also turn it round.

robot gripper

FAMOUS LIVES

KHUFU (c. 2900 BC) was an early king of Egypt who was also called Cheops. He ruled for 23 years, and the great pyramid of Gizeh was built for him. This was one of the Seven Wonders of the ancient world. It is 140 metres high, and even today it is still one of the world's largest stone structures.

RAMESES THE GREAT (1292–1225 BC) was the second Egyptian king of that name. He built a temple at Abu-Simbel that was hewn from solid rock. In recent years this was moved to a new site, when it was threatened by the floodwaters of the new Aswan Dam.

CYRUS THE GREAT (c. 600–529 BC) was the king of Anshan, within the empire of the Medes. In 553 BC he rebelled against his rulers. Four years later he had overthrown the Medes. By the time of his death he had created the first Persian Empire, which stretched from the Indus River in India to the shores of the eastern Mediterranean.

SIDDHARTHA GAUTAMA (563–484 BC) was an Indian prince who became world famous under the name of Buddha. The name means the 'awakened' or 'enlightened one'. According to legend, he left his wife and child to become a wandering religious beggar. He meditated for a long time, until he worked out ideas about freedom and self-knowledge. These ideas have become known as the 'way'. He spent most of his life preaching, and teaching his disciples and followers. Buddhism, the way of life taught by Buddha, became especially widespread in China.

AESCHYLUS (525–456 BC) is often called the 'father of Greek drama'. Out of the 90 or so tragedies that he wrote, only seven are still known. Two of the best known are *Prometheus Bound* and *Orestia*. Other famous Greek playwrights include Sophocles (496–406 BC) who wrote *Electra* and *Oedipus Rex*, and Euripides (c. 484–407 BC) who wrote the *Trojan Women*, *Medea*, and another version of the story of *Electra*. He brought realism to Greek drama. The subjects of these plays were the gods and heroes of Greek myths and legends. Their plays were performed in annual competitions at the Festival of Dionysus in Athens, at which prizes were given.

PERICLES (c. 490–429 BC) was a statesman of ancient Athens. Under his leadership the city-state prospered, and achieved its greatest power. In 469 he became the leader of the democratic party, and a few years later gained political control of the city. As a war general, he put down the revolt of Euboea and conquered Samos. Between 440 and 432 he set about making the public buildings of Athens the most beautiful of the time. He oversaw the building of the Parthenon on the Acropolis, a hill overlooking the city. When Athens went to war with Sparta in 431, Pericles said that Athens should rely on its sea power. His warning was not heeded, and Athens was led into disaster.

HERODOTUS (c. 484–424 BC) is often known as the 'father of history'. He spent 17 years of his early life travelling widely. When he began to write his history of the war between the Greeks and the Persians, he also studied the past. He looked for details that would make sense of the developments that led to the war. This attention to detail sets him apart from other historians of the time.

SOCRATES (469–399 BC) was the most famous Athenian thinker who ever lived. His teachings, however, led to him being condemned to death. Although Socrates wrote nothing himself, a great deal is known about him from his pupils, the most famous of whom was Plato. Socrates taught his pupils to think about things by questioning them. This questioning applied to everything, even laws. For this reason he was sentenced to death, and had to drink a cup of poisonous hemlock. His ideas have influenced philosophers ever since.

XENOPHON (c. 430–c. 356 BC) was an Athenian general who was exiled from the city for his friendship with Socrates. He wrote a history of Greece, and another history of his own military expeditions. Several of his works are about the life and the teachings of Socrates. Xenophon also wrote essays and stories.

ALEXANDER THE GREAT (356–323 BC) was a famous Greek general. In 336 BC he became the king of Macedon, a state to the north of Greece, and consolidated his control over the other Greek states conquered by his father, Phillip.
He then went on to conquer the empire of the Persians. He took Egypt, where he founded the great city of Alexandria. His army finally pushed as far east as India. Alexander died in Babylon, at the age of 33. His empire did not last long after he died, but it did much to spread the learning and way of life of the Greeks throughout the Middle East.

ARCHIMEDES (c. 287–c. 212 BC) was a Greek mathematician and an inventor. He discovered the principles by which levers work, and the principles by which objects float in water. He also invented the planetarium, and a screw pump that could be used to draw water.

CICERO (106–43 BC) was one of the greatest speakers, thinkers and statesmen of ancient Rome. His many letters to friends give us a remarkable and detailed view of life in his time. During the rule of Julius Caesar he stayed clear of politics. After Caesar's murder, however, Cicero sided with the republic. He was eventually put to death.

VIRGIL (70–19 BC) was a Roman poet who wrote the *Georgics*, poems which praise the life of peasants, and the *Aeneid*, an epic poem about the wanderings of a soldier after the war with Troy. Virgil was a friend of another writer called Horace, who wrote two volumes of *Satires* about the wickedness and the folly of mankind. Horace wrote other long poems too, which are still very much admired.

CLEOPATRA (69–30 BC) was a queen of Egypt. She was famous for her beauty and her political cleverness. At first she ruled jointly with her brother, who was also her husband, until she was driven out by him. Later she gained the support of the Roman leader Julius Caesar, who defeated her brother. She became

Caesar's mistress, and lived with him in Rome until returning to Egypt and taking up power again. Later she won the love of Mark Antony, another ruler of Rome. When she and Antony were defeated by Romans she killed herself, rather than be paraded in defeat through Rome. Legend claims that she died by being bitten by an asp, although it is more likely that she took poison.

AUGUSTUS (63 BC–AD 14) was the first emperor of Rome. His original name was Octavian, but he took the name Augustus after becoming the leader of Rome. He was the adopted son of Julius Caesar, and his heir after Caesar died in 45 BC. He defeated Antony and Cleopatra at the battle of Actium in 31 BC, and then became the sole ruler of Rome.

LIVY (59 BC–AD 17) was a Roman historian, who produced a massive account of the city's history. It totalled 142 books in all, although today most are missing. His work began with the founding of the city, and continued through to 9 BC.

JESUS CHRIST (c. 4 BC–c. 29 AD) was the founder of the Christian religion. The name 'Jesus' comes from the Hebrew word for 'saviour', and the name 'Christ' from the Greek for 'messiah'. He was born in Palestine, and spent his early days working as a carpenter. Later, as an adult, he preached in the area around Galilee, where he gathered disciples and was well received by ordinary people. He is said to have performed many miracles, and he defended the poor and oppressed against the privileged people of the time. Many of his followers thought him to be the son of God and the Messiah, but religious authorities of the time

suspected his activities. The Romans condemned him to death, and crucified him. Christians believe that he then rose from the dead and went to heaven.

TRAJAN (AD 53–117) was emperor during the time when the Roman empire grew to its greatest size. His military successes are commemorated by a column in the Forum in Rome. He was one of the greatest Roman leaders. He strengthened the empire by building roads, bridges, baths and libraries, and improving the water supplies.

ATTILA THE HUN (c. 400–453) was known in the ancient civilised world as the 'Scourge of God'. He led a great barbarian army out of Asia, and devastated the eastern Roman empire. Only the massive defences of Constantinople saved that city from being overrun. In the west he was stopped at the battle of Châlons in France, but he later turned and attacked Italy. He stopped short of Rome, after Pope Leo the Great paid him a huge ransom. The next year he died, probably after being poisoned, and his vast empire soon collapsed.

MOHAMMED (570–632) was the founder of the religion of Islam. He was born in Mecca, in Arabia, where he was at first a shepherd boy and then a merchant. At the age of 40 he realized that he had the calling to become a prophet. He began preaching that there was only one God, and began converting people to his own religious ideas. Later he turned to politics and proclaimed a new code of law. His activities made him many enemies, and he was forced to flee Mecca for Medina. Here he built up a following, and in 630 he returned to take

Mecca. Mohammed was then recognized as a prophet, and his power soon spread throughout Arabia. After his death in 632, his followers continued to spread his teachings. In the next two centuries Islam spread from the Atlantic in the west to southern Asia in the east.

CHARLEMAGNE (742–814) was one of the greatest rulers in Europe during the Middle Ages. He inherited the kingdom of the Franks from his father and brother. After a series of wars that lasted for 30 years, he subdued the Saxons and conquered Lombardy. He also fought against the Arabs in Spain, and against the Avars whom he finally defeated. On Christmas Day, in the year 800, he was crowned emperor of the Romans by Pope Leo III, thus founding the Holy Roman Empire. It lasted for 1000 years, until dismantled by Napoleon in 1806. Charlemagne encouraged Christianity in his lands, founded schools, and fostered art and literature. His empire fell apart after he died, because his son and grandsons divided it up between them.

SALADIN (1138–1193) was a Kurdish general who made himself Sultan of Egypt and Syria. He defeated the Crusaders at the battle of Hittin in 1187, and went on to take most of the Holy Land from the Christians. In October 1187 he took Jerusalem, after a 14-day siege. He next had to fight the European armies of the Third Crusade, led by Richard I of England and Philip II of France. The Crusaders almost reached Jerusalem, but were finally forced to make a truce with Saladin. At his death, his empire stretched from North Africa to the Tigris and from Armenia to the Indian Ocean. He was famous for his courage, courtesy and chivalry.

GENGHIS KHAN (1162–1227), meaning Khan of Khans, was the title taken by the greatest leader the Mongols ever had. He was a military genius, and made astonishing conquests in the 18 years of his power, though his armies are said to have killed over five million people. His empire reached from China to the River Volga, and from Siberia to India. It was held together by a far reaching postal system, a network of police, and a code of laws that is still in practice today in some parts of Asia.

GIÓTTO (c. 1266–1337) was an Italian painter and sculptor who is sometimes known as the 'father of Renaissance art'. He painted many religious frescos of the life of Christ and of the saints, and also did portraits. One of his subjects was the poet Dante. Giotto also worked as the chief architect of the cathedral of Florence, and designed the magnificent belltower known today as Giotto's Tower.

DANTE ALIGHIERI (1365–1321) was a great Italian poet. He was born and brought up in Florence. He studied in numerous university towns throughout Europe, and later became involved in Italian politics. In 1302, after being banished from Florence, he took up a wandering way of life. During this period he wrote a long poem called the *Divine Comedy*. It tells of his imaginary journey through Hell and Paradise. It is considered to be one of the great masterpieces of world literature. It tells of the world beyond death, and in so doing shows an enormous range and variety of human feelings.

JOAN OF ARC (1412–1431) was a French peasant girl. At the age of 13 she began hearing the voices of the angels Michael and Gabriel, and of the saints Catherine and Margaret. At first they simply directed her to lead a holy life. Later they urged her to save France by driving out the English, and crowning Charles, the young dauphin, as king. Through surprising persistence she persuaded Charles to give her a military command. Dressed in a suit of armour, she led her small army into war. She managed to break the siege of Orleans, and force the English to fall back. Afterwards she escorted Charles to his coronation as king at Reims cathedral. A year later, she was captured by Burgundians, and eventually sold to the English as a prisoner. She was charged with witchcraft, tried, and hastily sentenced. In May 1431 she was burned at the stake, in the old marketplace of Rouen. But in later years her sentence was overturned and she was declared innocent. In 1920, Pope Benedict XV declared her a saint.

CHRISTOPHER COLUMBUS (1451–1506) was a famous Italian adventurer. He led four expeditions across the Atlantic in the 1490s, to explore the New World and prove his theory that the world was round. From his point of view, the voyages were all failures. He believed that he could reach Japan and the East Indies by sailing westward around the world. Unfortunately, he underestimated the distance by two-thirds, and instead discovered the long-forgotten world of America. He explored the area of the Caribbean and Central America, never giving up hope that he would find a way to the East. His searches were unsuccessful, and he died neglected and in poverty. He still refused to believe that he had found a new continent, and not the Far East.

LEONARDO DA VINCI (1452–1519) was one of the most gifted men of the Renaissance. He is famous for his paintings, especially the portrait of *Mona Lisa* and the fresco called *The Last Supper*. But he also did sculpture and architecture, and was a skilled engineer and builder. He designed plans for tanks, submarines and flying machines that were centuries ahead of his time. He also made studies of the weather, the human body and mathematics. These contributed greatly to the knowledge of the time.

NICOLAUS COPERNICUS (1473–1543)

was a Polish doctor of medicine, a priest and an astronomer. It is as an astronomer that he is best known today. Because of his work in proving that the Earth spins on its own axis, and revolves around the Sun along with the other planets, he is considered to be the founder of modern astronomy. In his time, his ideas were so new and startling that he did not publish them until the year of his death. He feared that the Church and other authorities would ban his work for being too revolutionary.

ELIZABETH I (1533–1603) was the

daughter of Henry VIII, and became queen of England. She strengthened the position of the Protestant religion in the country, and her own position as head of the Church, while severely persecuting Catholics. Her policies toward Catholics led to the Spanish sending an armada to attack England, but it was defeated by the English navy and a lucky storm. Under Elizabeth's rule, England became a great world power.

WILLIAM SHAKESPEARE (1564–

1616) was the greatest playwright in the English language. He wrote 37 plays, as well as poetry, and his work is performed all over the world. Very little is known about his life, but his writing tells us that he was a genius with words and ideas. Some of his best-known plays are *Hamlet, Romeo and Juliet, King Lear*, and *The Tempest*. Shakespeare is also famous for his sonnets, which are a series of poems.

GALILEO (1564–1642) was an Italian

scientist and astronomer. He was one of the first thinkers to conduct experiments in a modern scientific way. He discovered the laws according to which a pendulum moves, and falling objects plunge to Earth, He was one of the first to build a telescope, and by his studies showed that Copernicus' ideas of the Universe were indeed true.

REMBRANDT VAN RIJN (1606–1669)

was a Dutch painter who became one of Europe's greatest artists. He settled in Amsterdam, where he became much in demand as a portrait painter. The year his wife died, 1642, marked a turning point in his fortunes. The demand for his works fell, and by 1656 he had become bankrupt. Yet his output was as great as ever throughout his last years of poverty and obscurity. Today, more than 600 paintings, 2000 drawings and 300 etchings survive as a monument to his genius.

ISAAC NEWTON (1642–1727) was one

of the most outstanding scientists who ever lived. His studies in mathematics, physics and astronomy gave rise to some of the most important insights into the way the Universe works. In a burst of inspired work, from 1665 to 1667, he explained the laws of gravitation, discovered the secrets of light and colour, and invented calculus. He was rewarded in his lifetime by being knighted.

JOHANN SEBASTIAN BACH (1685–

1750) was a German composer and organist. His work had an enormous influence on composers who followed him. He wrote a huge amount of music including three passions, five masses, 29 concerts, and over 200 church cantatas.

GEORGE FREDERICK HANDEL (1685–1759), a German-born composer, became a British subject in 1726. He achieved great fame and popularity there. Handel wrote chamber music, operas and organ music, as well as music for full orchestras. He was much admired by other composers such as Mozart and Beethoven.

BENJAMIN FRANKLIN (1706–1790) was one of the most active American thinkers ever to have lived. In his lifetime he was a printer, publisher, writer, scientist, postmaster, diplomat and statesman. He founded Philadelphia's first public library, its first fire insurance company, its first hospital and university. He discovered the Atlantic Gulf Stream, and the electrical nature of lightning. He helped to draw up America's Declaration of Independence, and his last public act was to sign a message to Congress asking it to discourage slavery.

JAMES WATT (1736–1819) was a Scottish inventor, who created the world's first efficient steam engine. He later manufactured these in Birmingham, England, with much success. His engines powered much of the machinery of the Industrial Revolution.

WOLFGANG AMADEUS MOZART (1756–1791) was an Austrian composer. He began writing music at the very young age of five, under his father's direction. At six he went on his first concert tour. During his lifetime he produced over 600 works, including two very famous operas, *Don Giovanni* and *The Magic Flute*. His work was much admired, but even so, continual money worries led to overwork, and he died before his 36th birthday.

NAPOLEON BONAPARTE (1769–1821) began his career as an unknown Corsican artillery officer. He rose to become emperor of the French, and the ruler of Europe. He was a brilliant general and at the head of the French armies he was able to dominate every European rival for 20 years. He was finally defeated at the Battle of Waterloo in 1815, and exiled to the island of St Helena.

LUDWIG VAN BEETHOVEN (1770–1827) lived most of his life in Vienna, where he worked as a composer and studied briefly with Mozart. He refused to be supported by a patron, and lived by teaching, performing and composing music. He had trouble with his hearing, and became totally deaf by 1819. Nevertheless, he continued to compose music until his death eight years later.

KARL MARX (1818–1883) was a German philosopher. He developed his ideas about socialism in Germany, and then later in exile in Paris and London. His work and writings appealed to many people, especially to workers in countries where the Industrial Revolution was most advanced. His influence since his death has been enormous, and has been felt in every country in the world.

FLORENCE NIGHTINGALE (1820–1919) was an English nurse and reformer. She created a sensation by taking a group of nurses to the battlefields of the Crimean War. Her work in caring for the sick and wounded led to proper medical care being introduced, for the first time, into army life.

LOUIS PASTEUR (1822–1895) was a French chemist, whose discoveries transformed chemistry and medicine. He found that tiny organisms, or bacteria, cause milk to ferment and were essential in making wine and beer. He thought that certain diseases were caused by microscopic germs invading and spreading throughout the body. He developed a way of fighting these germs by inoculating people. Two inoculations that he developed were for rabies and anthrax.

MARIE CURIE (1867–1934) was born in Poland. She was always interested in science, and travelled to Paris to study it further. There she met a physics teacher, called Pierre Curie, and married him. The Curies worked together on many experiments. In 1898 they discovered a new element, called radium. They shared a Nobel Prize for this work. Later, after Pierre died, Marie won another Nobel Prize for more work she did in chemistry.

MOHANDAS KARAMCHAND GANDHI (1869–1948) was the Hindu leader who could be considered the 'father of modern India'. He became a barrister during his studies in Britain. Then he returned home, to lead the fight for Indian independence from the English. In support for home rule he organized his famous campaigns of passive resistance and non-cooperation with the English. His work inspired huge support, and led to India being granted its independence in 1947.

NIKOLAI LENIN (1870–1924) was a Russian politician. He led the Bolshevik party which, in November 1917, overthrew the weakened Russian government. This revolution began the modern country called the USSR. Lenin was highly influenced by the socialist ideas of Karl Marx. He established the control of the Communist Party over the political affairs of Russia, and became the country's leader until his death in 1924. His books and ideas are still studied today.

WINSTON CHURCHILL (1874–1965) was a British statesman who led the country during World War II. He became Prime Minister in 1940, just as European resistance to Germany was collapsing. He worked hard to persuade the United States to support Britain and enter the war, and established close ties with President Roosevelt. He inspired his country with some of the finest speeches in its history, and is remembered with much affection.

ADOLF HITLER (1889–1945) was an Austrian. He became leader of the German Nazi Party in 1920, and leader of the country in 1933. Under his guidance Germany embarked on a war with the rest of Europe, that created a catastrophe of unprecedented scale. During World War II more than 50 million people died. In 1945, Hitler committed suicide in Berlin, as Allied armies moved into the city.

RULERS OF ENGLAND

Saxons

Egbert	827–839
Ethelwulf	839–858
Ethelbald	858–860
Ethelbert	860–866
Ethelred I	866–871
Alfred the Great	871–899
Edward the Elder	899–924
Athelstan	924–939
Edmund	939–946
Edred	946–955
Edwy	955–959
Edgar	959–975
Edward the Martyr	975–978
Ethelred the Unready	978–1016
Edmund Ironside	1016

Danes

Canute	1016–1035
Harold I Harefoot	1035–1040
Hardicanute	1040–1042

Saxons

Edward the Confessor	1042–1066
Harold II	1066

House of Normandy

William the Conqueror	1066–1087
William II	1087–1100
Henry I	1100–1135
Stephen	1135–1154

House of Plantagenet

Henry II	1154–1189
Richard I	1189–1199
John	1199–1216
Henry III	1216–1272
Edward I	1272–1307
Edward II	1307–1327
Edward III	1327–1377
Richard II	1377–1399

House of Lancaster

Henry IV	1399–1413
Henry V	1413–1422
Henry VI	1422–1461

House of York

Edward IV	1461–1483
Edward V	1483
Richard III	1483–1485

House of Tudor

Henry VII	1485–1509
Henry VIII	1509–1547
Edward VI	1547–1553
Mary I	1553–1558
Elizabeth I	1558–1603

RULERS OF SCOTLAND

Malcolm II	1005–1034
Duncan I	1034–1040
Macbeth (usurper)	1040–1057
Malcolm III Canmore	1057–1093
Donald Bane	1093–1094
Duncan II	1094
Donald Bane	1094–1097
Edgar	1097–1107
Alexander I	1107–1124
David I	1124–1153
Malcolm IV	1153–1165
William the Lion	1165–1214
Alexander II	1214–1249
Alexander III	1249–1286
Margaret of Norway	1286–1290
(*interregnum 1290–1292*)	
John Balliol	1292–1296
(*interregnum 1296–1306*)	
Robert I (Bruce)	1306–1329
David II	1329–1371

House of Stuart

Robert II	1371–1390
Robert III	1390–1406
James I	1406–1437
James II	1437–1460
James III	1460–1488
James IV	1488–1513
James V	1513–1542
Mary	1542–1567
James VI	1567–1625

(Became James I of Great Britain in 1603)

RULERS OF GREAT BRITAIN

House of Stuart

James I	1603–1625
Charles I	1625–1649
(*Commonwealth 1649–1658*)	

House of Stuart (restored)

Charles II	1660–1685
James II	1685–1688
William III } jointly	1689–1702
Mary II	1689–1694
Anne	1702–1714

House of Hanover

George I	1714–1727
George II	1727–1760
George III	1760–1820
George IV	1820–1830
William IV	1830–1837
Victoria	1837–1901

House of Saxe-Coburg

Edward VII	1901–1910

House of Windsor

George V	1910–1936
Edward VIII	1936
George VI	1936–1952
Elizabeth II	1952–

Transport & Travel

SHIPS

Nobody knows who invented boats. It happened long before people learned to draw or write, and probably began with somebody jumping onto a floating log or branch, perhaps to escape from a wild animal. Later, people discovered how to travel across water in greater safety and comfort on a raft. Made from a bundle or platform of logs or reeds tied together, this would carry people, goods and animals across rivers and lakes. They also invented a faster craft which was easier to control, the dug-out canoe. This is made by hollowing a log or tree trunk.

Early Explorers

The size of dug-outs is limited by the trees available, but in spite of this seafarers from the Pacific islands Hawaii and Tahiti crossed thousands of kilometres of open ocean and discovered New Zealand in dug-out canoes. Their voyages took place about 1,000 years ago. Long before then seamen had discovered ways of building much larger craft. The ancient Egyptians were probably the first people to venture out to sea. Around 1500 BC they sailed down the coast of Africa in ships built from brick-like blocks of wood. Their craft were not very strong or seaworthy, and had to be held together with thick ropes. But soon shipwrights worked out the basic method of boat and ship building which has been used ever since.

Building Methods

First a frame or skeleton is constructed. This has a strong backbone along the bottom of the boat, the keel; curved ribs forming the sides; and sturdy posts at the bow and stern. The frame is then covered with planks. With this framed and planked system, boats could be built much larger than before. They were also faster, easier to handle and more seaworthy. By ancient Roman times, roomy 'round ships' carried cargoes around the Mediterranean Sea and as far afield as Britain. Their merchant ships are called 'round' because they were tubby, and to contrast them with 'longships'—long narrow fighting galleys propelled by several banks of oars.

In later times Vikings from Scandinavia fitted sails to the longship, and used it for voyages of trade and exploration as well as for war.

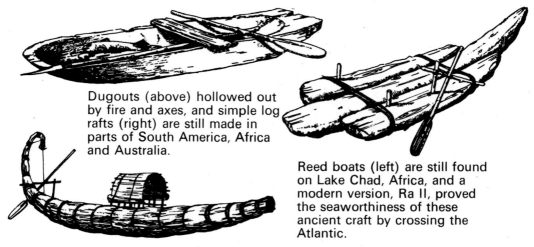

Dugouts (above) hollowed out by fire and axes, and simple log rafts (right) are still made in parts of South America, Africa and Australia.

Reed boats (left) are still found on Lake Chad, Africa, and a modern version, Ra II, proved the seaworthiness of these ancient craft by crossing the Atlantic.

Ocean-going Ships

By around 1450 the sleek lines of the longship and the tubby shape of the round ship merged in a new type of vessel, the carrack. This was much bigger than its ancestors. It had several decks, with storage and living space between them. It had short quarter and half decks built on top of the main hull. And it had several masts and many sails. Most of these were square sails, set across the ship. They work best when the wind blows from behind. But some were fore-and-aft sails. These are set along the line of the hull, and they allow ships to make progress in any wind.

The carracks, and their sleeker and faster successor, the galleon, were the first true ocean-going ships, and during the great Age of Discovery between about 1450 and 1550 explorers voyaged all over the world. Vasco da Gama sailed around Africa to India; Christopher Columbus crossed the Atlantic to America; and Ferdinand Magellan sailed right round the world.

Steam-powered Ships

During the following 250 years ship design changed little. Then the steam engine was invented and adapted to power ships. At last people could travel the oceans without having to rely on the wind. And soon afterwards shipwrights realized that they could build larger, stronger and faster ships out of metal. The modern era of shipping and sea travel had begun, and by 1850 luxurious liners carried travellers across the oceans in comfort and—usually—in safety.

For some time many cargoes continued to be transported around the world in huge, tall-masted sailing ships. But by 1930 these had given way to a wide range of powered cargo ships, and today there

Above: A reconstruction of the *Santa Maria*, one of the ships in which Columbus first crossed the Atlantic in 1492. The voyage took 36 days. The *Santa Maria* was a small carrack with raised decks at bow and stern. The fore and main masts had square sails, while the triangular sail on the third mast was a fore-and-aft sail.

Below: The *Victory*, Admiral Nelson's flagship at the battle of Trafalgar, 1805. She was basically little different from the fighting galleons of the time of the Spanish Armada, and had a top speed of around 17 km/h.

Hovercraft (far right) and hydrofoils (below) are flying ships. They skim just above the water, and can therefore travel much faster than ordinary ships. The hovercraft travels at 140 km/h, the hydrofoil at around 100 km/h. Hovercraft ride on a cushion of air, and hydrofoils on underwater wings.

are specialized types of merchant ship for all sorts of goods.

Supertankers

Biggest of all are the giant supertankers. These can measure up to 400 metres in length, and carry half a million tonnes of oil. Yet they need a crew of only 30 men— fewer than a sailing merchant ship carrying a few hundred tonnes. Like most modern ships, they are packed with electronic equipment which checks the running of the engines and the conditions of the cargo, and even keeps the ship on course.

Supertankers are powered by vast steam turbine engines, but most other ships have diesel engines similar to those used in buses and trains. Tankers are a kind of 'bulk ship'—they carry just one cargo in bulk. Others include ore carriers; ships transporting grain, sugar,

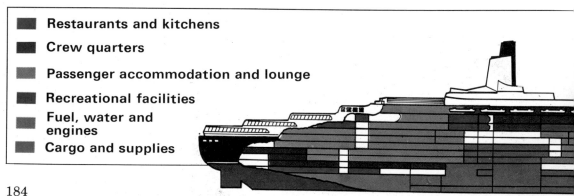

■ Restaurants and kitchens

■ Crew quarters

■ Passenger accommodation and lounge

■ Recreational facilities

■ Fuel, water and engines

■ Cargo and supplies

A large passenger-carrying hovercraft

wine, and gas; and container ships. Containers are large standard-sized boxes, and may be loaded with almost anything. Their great advantage is that they make loading and unloading a ship very easy. General cargo ships take weeks to load and unload. A container ship takes just a day and a half.

Fifty years ago passenger liners were the queens of the oceans. Today, most travellers prefer to fly, and it is the cargo ships that dominate the sea. They carry raw materials, finished products, food and fuel around the world. Because they have to push their way through the water, which is 800 times as dense or thick as air, ships are slow. Few travel faster than 40 km/h. But they are large, and can carry freight much more cheaply than aeroplanes.

Above: The *Sirius*, the first steam ship to cross the Atlantic mainly by steam power, 1838. The voyage took 18 days 10 hours.
Below left: The *Queen Elizabeth 2*, the world's largest passenger liner. She carries over 2,000 passengers.
Below: The *Titanic*, a giant luxury liner that struck an iceberg and sank in 1912.

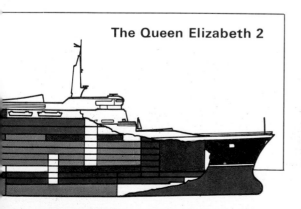

The Queen Elizabeth 2

TRAINS AND RAILWAYS

Trains run on metal wheels along smooth metal tracks. The wheels roll very smoothly, as there is very little friction. So much less power is needed than for driving road vehicles. Trains provide the best way of transporting large and heavy loads on land.

The idea of railways was invented by the ancient Greeks, who cut grooves or 'rutways' in rocky tracks so that their carts would roll more smoothly. Around 1500 years later, wagon-ways were invented. These were raised wooden tracks used in coal mines for wagons to travel along. The first metal rails were made in 1789, and all that was needed to begin the railway age was a locomotive—an engine to haul wagons and coaches.

The First Locomotives
The first steam locomotive was built by the English engineer Richard Trevithick in 1803, and the first steam powered public railway opened in 1825. This was the Stockton and Darlington Railway in north-east England. In 1829 a competition was held to find a faster and more reliable locomotive for the new Liverpool and Manchester Railway. Only one locomotive successfully completed the trials, and it became the most famous ever. It was Stephenson's *Rocket*.

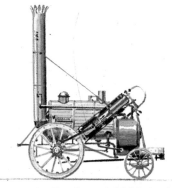

Stephenson's *Rocket* of 1829 had a top speed of 47 km/h.

Railway record-breakers: the world's fastest steam locomotive, the *Mallard*, reached a speed of 203 km/h in 1938; the most powerful, an American *Mallet*, hauled goods trains two kilometres long; and the largest, the Union Pacific *Big Boy*, weighed 500 tonnes with its tender.

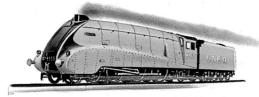

Mallard

Mallet

Big Boy

This French electric train is the world record holder on ordinary tracks. In 1955 it reached 330.9 km/h.

The Railway Age

Soon railways were built in other countries, and for the first time in the world's history ordinary people could travel around easily and cheaply. Before the arrival of trains, the only ways of travelling were on foot or by horse.

The first trains seemed very fast to people at the time, but by our standards they were slow. Trevithick's first locomotive reached 15 km/h, while the *Rocket* hauling a load of wagons could keep up a steady 35 km/h. But they were the fastest means of transport in the world, a record

they kept for nearly 100 years. Engineers soon built faster trains, and by 1900 speeds had risen to almost 200 km/h.

The golden age of steam trains lasted until the 1940s, and included the fastest steam train of all time, the streamlined *Mallard*, and the largest and heaviest locomotives, the American Big Boys. *Mallard's* record, achieved in 1938, was 203 km/h, a speed even today reached by few trains. The Big Boys were two locomotives in one, and had eight pairs of driving wheels. Designed to haul express freight trains on mountainous routes,

Aérotrain, an experimental hovertrain with aircraft engines.

they reached about 115 km/h pulling as many as 70 wagons—and burning up to 22 tonnes of coal an hour.

Modern Trains

Steam trains suffer from many disadvantages. They are dirty and inefficient, burning fuel wastefully. It takes hours for them to build up steam.

Today most railways use diesel, electric and gas turbine trains. They are cleaner and cheaper to run. Electric trains are the cleanest and quietest of all, and the fastest and most powerful. This is because they carry no fuel, and no engines to convert fuel into power. Their power comes ready made, and they just need quite small electric motors. But setting up extra rails or wires to carry the electricity along the track is very expensive. So electric power is usually reserved for very busy routes.

Elsewhere diesel trains do most of the work, except where extra speed is needed. Then gas turbine locomotives can provide faster services. Their engines are like those in jet aircraft, but they are used to turn the wheels, not for jet propulsion.

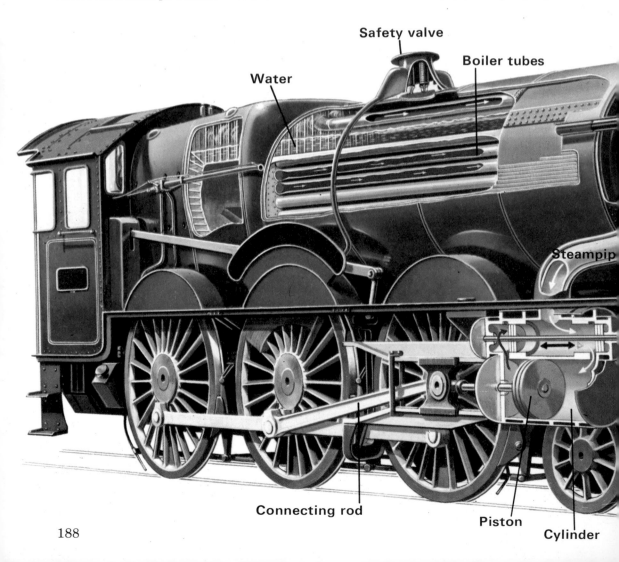

Safety valve

Boiler tubes

Water

Steampip

Connecting rod

Piston

Cylinder

Both gas turbine and electric trains have reached speeds over 300 km/h.

There are plans for much faster trains, held just off the track and propelled by magnetic power. These should bring inter-city services at almost 500 km/h. And because they have no moving parts and little friction, they will be smooth and almost silent.

Firebox

Above: Britain's Advanced Passenger Train (APT). It travels at up to 245 km/h, and has coaches which tilt when the train rounds bends at speed. This helps to keep the train on the track, and to give passengers a comfortable ride.
Left: Inside a steam locomotive. The fire heats water in the boiler tubes to make steam. The steam forces the piston back and forth in the cylinder. The piston is linked to the driving wheels by a connecting rod which turns the wheels.

ROAD TRANSPORT

When the first men wanted to transport a heavy load they put it on a kind of sledge and dragged it along. Later they used animals to haul the sledge, and perhaps they found that placing logs or poles under the sledge made it easier to pull along. Then, about 6000 years ago, someone dreamed up the most important invention in the entire story of transport—the wheel. Now people could build carts, and haul heavier loads more easily. And they built roads to make travel still better. For several thousand years road transport changed little. Coaches and carriages were improved by fitting swivelling front wheels for steering and springs to cushion them from rough roads. But travelling by road 200 years ago was much the same as 2000 years earlier.

People dreamed of a 'horseless carriage' moved along by its own power, but they had no engine. They tried using wind power, fitting carts with sails, kites and even windmills. The scientist Isaac Newton built a toy 'car' propelled by a jet of steam, and engineers wondered if they could build full-sized clockwork vehicles. But none of these ideas really worked. In those days wealthy people had fine houses, beautiful furniture and delicately engineered clocks. But if they wanted to travel they still had to rely on horse-drawn carriages which lumbered over rough roads at an average speed of only 6 km/h.

Road Power

Then at last the first engine was invented, the steam engine, and in 1769 the world's first engine-powered road vehicle was tried out. It is illustrated at the top of the facing page. Built by the French engineer Nicholas Cugnot to carry a gun, it had a massive wooden frame, and a boiler perched out ahead of the front wheel. It was difficult to control; it was slow (5 km/h); it had to stop every 15 minutes to build up steam; and it ended by crashing into a wall. But it was a beginning, and before long other inventors and engineers made improved steam cars.

The first really successful ones were built by Richard Trevithick in 1801 and 1803, just before he produced the world's first railway locomotive. The first, 'Captain Dick's Puffer', climbed a hill in his home village, while the second steamed around London and carried eight passengers.

A brief era of steam coaches followed, but before long the companies who ran horse-drawn coach services, and the new railways, forced the new invention off the roads. They argued that steam power was dangerous, and that it cost more than horse power. In fact the steam coaches were faster and cheaper to run than their rivals.

A few well-to-do people built steam cars or 'horseless carriages'. But for the most part people just were not interested in the invention. They were frightened by it. But more important, few people wanted cars. The wealthy were content to travel in their splendid horse-drawn coaches. Others either did not have the money, or the time. They had never travelled far from home and they did not particularly want to.

Pedal Power

However, before long another invention appeared which cost little, and which gave people a taste for driving around. This was the bicycle. It seems strange that this simple and efficient means of transport was not invented hundreds of

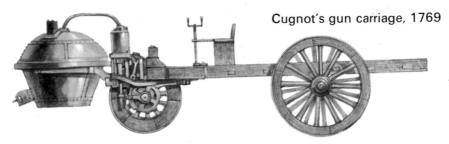

Cugnot's gun carriage, 1769

years earlier. But in fact the bicycle was invented in 1790, 21 years after Cugnot's steam gun carriage. The first bicycles were sometimes called hobby horses or dandy horses. They had no pedals. The rider walked his machine along with his feet on the ground. The pedal bicycle was invented by a Scottish blacksmith in 1839, and by the 1860s and 1870s there was a bicycle craze. For the first time ordinary people discovered the fun of getting out and about and seeing the countryside. Suddenly people grew interested in the almost forgotten invention of 50 years earlier, the car.

Motor Cars

In spite of lack of interest, engineers had been working on new types of car during these 50 years, and they had developed a new type of engine. It ran on petrol or gas, and was called by one early inventor an 'explosion engine'. We call it the 'internal combustion engine', because the combustion or burning takes place inside the cylinder. The explosion pushes the piston down in the cylinder. There is a fuel system to inject fuel into the cylinder, and an ignition system to set fire to it.

The push of steam on a piston is slow, steady and immensely powerful. It can start a whole train moving with ease. The push of exploding petrol on an internal combustion engine's piston is sharp, sudden and not very powerful. Because of

A 1909 Rolls Royce Silver Ghost, an early super-car. It cost a fortune, but lasted a lifetime, unlike most cars today which wear out in a few years.

these differences petrol engines must have several cylinders and pistons to produce a smooth flow of power. They must drive the wheels through a clutch— a device which connects the engine to the wheels gradually and gently. And they need gears.

Unlike steam, petrol engines only generate useful power when they are running quite quickly. Gears allow a fast running engine to turn the wheels slowly and powerfully, for starting off and climbing hills. They also enable it to turn the wheels more quickly, but with less power, for cruising along a level road. The clutch, gears and shafts which take the engine's power to the actual road wheels are together called the transmission system. In addition, cars have a cooling system to stop the engine getting too hot; a steering system to turn the front wheels; an electrical system to power the lights and electrical gadgets and the ignition system; a lubrication system to keep all moving parts oiled and running smoothly; a suspension system,

consisting of springs and shock absorbers, to cushion the car and its passengers from bumps and holes in the road; and a braking system.

Modern Cars

The first petrol cars were built by the German engineers Karl Benz and Gottleib Daimler in 1885 and 1886. For around 20 years most cars were difficult to start, uncomfortable, unreliable and noisy. Driving was an adventure, with frequent breakdowns and occasional attacks by

A modern long distance racing car, the Porsche 936. In 1977 it averaged 193.6 km/h in the Le Mans 24 hour race.

dogs and hostile pedestrians. There was also no protection from the weather. But by 1910 engineers had improved the mechanical aspects, designers had evolved enclosed and often luxurious bodywork, and Henry Ford had pioneered the production line.

This method of mass-producing cars enabled him to lower his prices. This brought in the era of popular motoring, which has changed our lives completely. It has brought countless people around the world freedom and enjoyment undreamed of 100 years ago. But it has also brought mammoth traffic jams, thousands of accidents, and vast quantities of poisonous exhaust fumes.

Today, car designers are working on ways to make cars cleaner, safer and more economical. They make the body stronger, to protect occupants in a crash. They fit two braking systems, so that if one fails the other can still stop the car. They fit electronic devices to control the ignition and save fuel. And they are even beginning to fit mini-computers and electronic eyes, to tell the driver if he gets too close to the car in front, to tell him about traffic jams ahead, and to check the condition of the engine and other systems. Perhaps in the future robots will actually drive our cars for us.

Above: The Blue Flame, holder of the world land speed record from 1970 until 1979. It reached an amazing 1,016 km/h. Below: Racing cyclists. Cycling is the fastest man-powered sport. The speed record stands at 78 km/h.

AIR TRAVEL

The first sizeable powered aeroplane was called a carriage. Designed by William Henson and built in 1842–3, the Aerial Steam Carriage is today in London's Science Museum. It looked much more like an aeroplane than the Flyer illustrated on this page, but it never left the ground. There was no engine light enough at the time.

Almost since the beginning of history inventor had wondered how they could imitate the flight of birds. Some even built themselves wings, and leaped to their deaths from high cliffs.

Wings covered with fabric——

4-cylinder liquid-cooled —— 12HP Wright engine

Twin steering rudders——

Flying Machines

By the early 1800s a few scientists had worked out that flying machines were possible. But as they had no suitable engines, they could only test their ideas on kites and model gliders. These fly in the same way. Air rushing over the curved upper side of the wing creates a lifting force, which makes it fly. Gliders have to be launched or thrown up to get air flowing over the wings, while with kites the wind does the job. Aeroplanes, on the other hand, have engines which move them forwards. As they build up speed along the ground, the flow of air creates the lift which gets them airborne.

During the fifty years following the Aerial Steam Carriage, many inventors tried building steam powered planes. A few hopped briefly off the ground, but no more. Other pioneers decided that the most important thing was to learn to fly. Then they could look for an engine.

The Wright Brothers

In America two brothers, Wilbur and Orville Wright, built and flew a series of kites and gliders. By then the car and the petrol engine had been invented. When the Wright brothers had learned to fly their gliders they built a larger craft with a petrol engine. The Wright *Flyer* made the world's first controlled powered flight in 1903. The *Flyer* (above) looks to us as though it is flying backwards. The rudder is in front and the propellers push it along from behind. But it worked, and by 1905 the Wrights' *Flyer III* was making 40-kilometre flights at about 40 km/h.

Inventors in Europe followed with equally strange machines. One had wings like a venetian blind. Another had drum-shaped wings. But by 1909 aeroplanes had begun to look much as they do today—with a propeller at the front, one or two pairs of wings, and fins at the back. The upright tail fin is a rudder, for steering. The horizontal tail fins are elevators. They are angled to make the plane fly up or down. In addition to these adjustable control surfaces on the tail, aeroplanes have hinged flaps on the wings called

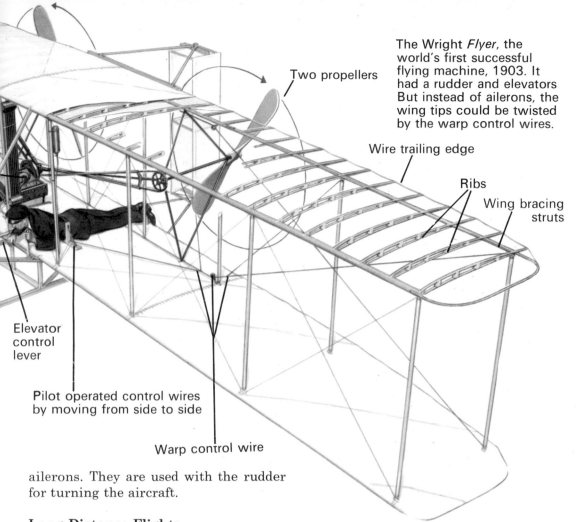

Two propellers

The Wright *Flyer*, the world's first successful flying machine, 1903. It had a rudder and elevators But instead of ailerons, the wing tips could be twisted by the warp control wires.

Wire trailing edge

Ribs

Wing bracing struts

Elevator control lever

Pilot operated control wires by moving from side to side

Warp control wire

ailerons. They are used with the rudder for turning the aircraft.

Long Distance Flights

At first aeroplanes were flown mainly for fun, and aerial circuses were popular. The aircraft were slow, small, flimsy and not very reliable. But soon people realized that they might one day be useful for transport, and an era of pioneering long distance flights began.

In 1909 the Frenchman Louis Blériot was the first to fly across the English Channel. But the flights that really excited the world were those across the Atlantic between America and Europe. First across non-stop were Alcock and Brown in a World War I bomber, in 1919.

And when Charles Lindbergh flew alone from New York to Paris in 1927 a crowd of 100,000 was there to cheer him.

Airline Companies

By then airlines had begun flying regular services over fairly short distances. But there were still no aircraft built for long range flights. Lindbergh's *Spirit of St Louis* had to be specially adapted for his 5810-kilometre trip. For a while people thought that long ocean crossings would have to be made by flying boats, huge

195

A Boeing Stratocruiser of the early 1950s. One of the first airliners that could cross oceans, it carried up to 89 passengers, and had some sleeping berths (left).

luxury airliners which could land in the ocean and refuel from ships. During the 1930s flying boats carried passengers across the oceans, and to most parts of the world. Then, during World War II, long range bombers and transport aircraft were improved. At the end of the war in 1945 they were put to peaceful use, flying passengers and freight across the world.

The Jet Age

The Comet, the first jet airliner, entered service in 1952. Jet engines move planes forward by thrusting air out backwards. They enable aircraft to fly much faster and much higher. Early jet airliners like the Comet and the Caravelle halved journey times on long-distance routes, and today's jets cruise at between 900 and 1,000 km/h. This is almost as fast as the speed at which sound travels. At the speed of sound, air in front of a plane piles up in a 'sound barrier'.

Special supersonic (faster than sound) aircraft are needed to get through this barrier. They must be extra well stream-lined and powerful, and they have swept back wings. Concorde, an Anglo-French supersonic airliner, cruises at 2,170 km/h and flies at an altitude of up to 18 km.

Since the start of the jet age airliners have become ever faster and ever larger. Today's giants of the sky like the Boeing 747 Jumbo Jet can carry almost 500 passengers in great comfort.

The 747 is the world's largest airliner. Between this and ordinary airliners come the wide-bodied airbuses. They carry around 300 passengers, and are mainly used on short or medium length journeys.

Tomorrow, yet larger airliners may be built, and there are schemes for 'hypersonic' craft flying at over 30,000 km/h.

Helicopters

Helicopters are fairly slow, but they need no airport or runway, and are useful for

The McDonnell Douglas DC-10, 1971, a jet airbus with three engines, a range of around 4,400 kilometres, and seating for over 300 passengers.

The European A 300 B Airbus, 1974. Like the DC-10 above it carries over 300 passengers, but it is designed for shorter journeys—for example between European cities.

Concorde, a delta winged supersonic airliner carrying up to 140 passengers. Its nose droops down to give the pilot a good view on landing and take-off.

197

short inter-city services, and for search and rescue tasks.

Aeroplanes have fixed wings. Helicopters have spinning wings called rotors. The rotor is rather like a huge propeller, but it is mounted on top of the craft, and lifts it straight up into the air. Once airborne, the rotor can be tilted slightly to propel the helicopter forwards—or backwards or sideways. Most helicopters also have a small rotor at the tail. This is to stop the whole craft being spun round by the main rotor. The helicopter's great advantage is that it lands and takes off vertically. But rotor-craft cannot fly very fast. Most have a top speed of less than 350 km/h. Aircraft designers try to combine some of the advantages of helicopters with the speed of fixed wing planes in STOL aeroplanes. The initials stand for Short Take Off and Landing. STOL aircraft are useful in remote areas where there are no long runways. They can also fly from small city airports.

In addition there are countless light aircraft. These are small planes used for example by farmers and flying doctors, as taxis, and of course for fun and sport.

The Boeing 747 airliner can carry up to 490 passengers but the basic passenger model shown here usually carries only 374 people. The spacious cabins provide plenty of room for all the passengers.

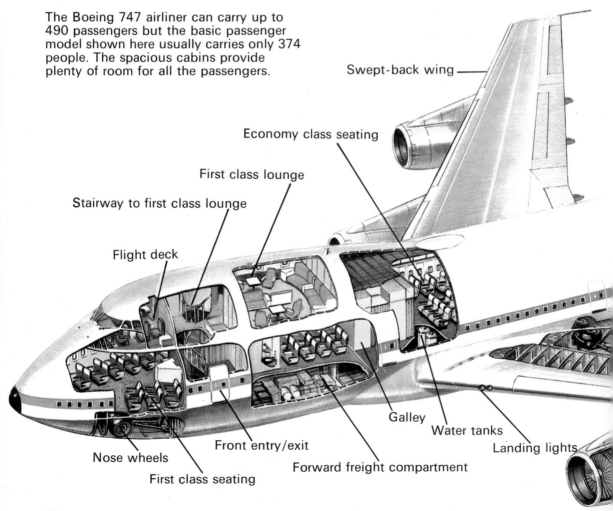

Swept-back wing

Economy class seating

First class lounge

Stairway to first class lounge

Flight deck

Galley

Water tanks

Landing lights

Nose wheels

First class seating

Front entry/exit

Forward freight compartment

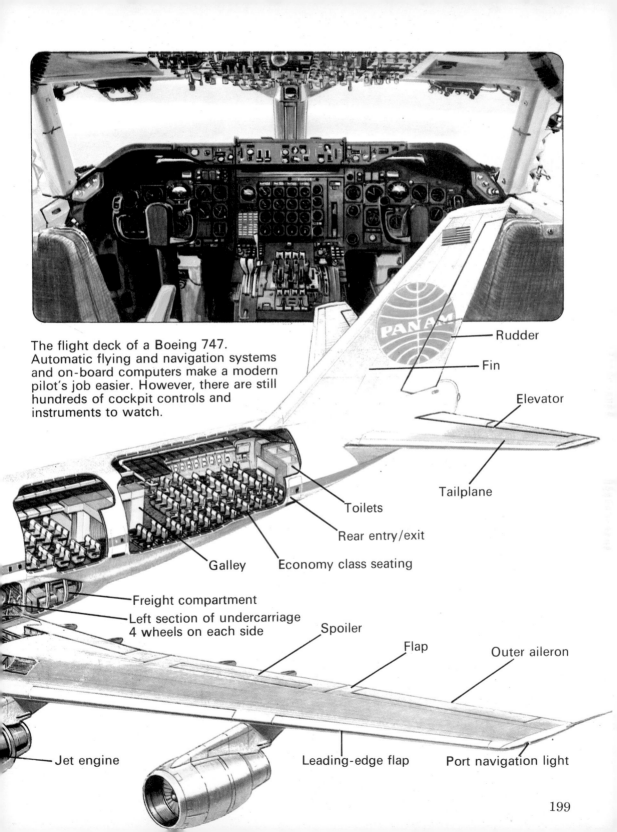

The flight deck of a Boeing 747.
Automatic flying and navigation systems
and on-board computers make a modern
pilot's job easier. However, there are still
hundreds of cockpit controls and
instruments to watch.

Rudder

Fin

Elevator

Tailplane

Toilets

Rear entry/exit

Economy class seating

Galley

Freight compartment

Left section of undercarriage
4 wheels on each side

Spoiler

Flap

Outer aileron

Jet engine

Leading-edge flap

Port navigation light

Winnie Mae
**first solo
flight round
the world, 1933**

USS Triton, **1960**

Magellan's ship
Vittoria, **1519–21**

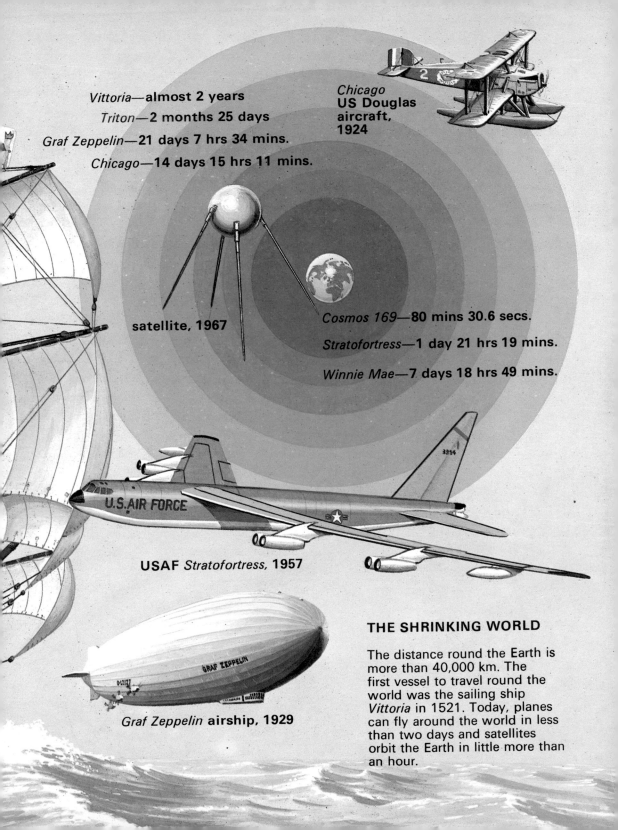

Vittoria—almost 2 years
Triton—2 months 25 days
Graf Zeppelin—21 days 7 hrs 34 mins.
Chicago—14 days 15 hrs 11 mins.

Chicago
US Douglas aircraft, 1924

satellite, 1967

Cosmos 169—80 mins 30.6 secs.
Stratofortress—1 day 21 hrs 19 mins.
Winnie Mae—7 days 18 hrs 49 mins.

USAF *Stratofortress*, **1957**

Graf Zeppelin **airship, 1929**

THE SHRINKING WORLD

The distance round the Earth is more than 40,000 km. The first vessel to travel round the world was the sailing ship *Vittoria* in 1521. Today, planes can fly around the world in less than two days and satellites orbit the Earth in little more than an hour.

INTERNATIONAL IDENTIFICATION LETTERS ON MOTOR CARS

A	Austria	GCA	Guatemala	RC	China (Taiwan)
ADN	Yemen	GH	Ghana	RCA	Central African
AFG	Afghanistan	GR	Greece		Republic
AL	Albania	GUY	Guyana	RCB	Congo
AND	Andorra			RCH	Chile
AUS	Australia	H	Hungary	RH	Haiti
		HK	Hong Kong	RI	Indonesia
B	Belgium	HKJ	Jordan	RIM	Mauritania
BDS	Barbados			RL	Lebanon
BG	Bulgaria	I	Italy	RM	Madagascar
BH	Belize	IL	Israel	RMM	Mali
BR	Brazil	IND	India	ROK	South Korea
BRN	Bahrain	IR	Iran	RP	Philippines
BRU	Brunei	IRL	Ireland, Republic of	RSM	San Marino
BS	Bahamas	IRQ	Iraq	RU	Burundi
BUR	Burma	IS	Iceland	RWA	Rwanda
C	Cuba	J	Japan		
CDN	Canada	JA	Jamaica	S	Sweden
CH	Switzerland			SD	Swaziland
CI	Ivory Coast	K	Khmer Republic	SF	Finland
CL	Sri Lanka	KWT	Kuwait	SGP	Singapore
CO	Colombia			SME	Surinam
CR	Costa Rica	L	Luxembourg	SN	Senegal
CS	Czechoslovakia	LAO	Laos	SU	USSR
CY	Cyprus	LAR	Libya	SY	Seychelles
		LB	Liberia	SYR	Syria
D	West Germany	LS	Lesotho		
DDR	East Germany			T	Thailand
DK	Denmark	M	Malta	TG	Togo
DOM	Dominican Republic	MA	Morocco	TN	Tunisia
DY	Dahomey	MAL	Malaysia	TR	Turkey
DZ	Algeria	MC	Monaco	TT	Trinidad and Tobago
		MEX	Mexico		
E	Spain (including	MS	Mauritius	U	Urguay
	provinces)	MW	Malawi	USA	United States
EAK	Kenya				
EAT	Tanzania	N	Norway	V	Vatican City
EAU	Uganda	NA	Netherlands Antilles	VN	Vietnam
EC	Ecuador	NIC	Nicaragua		
ET	Egypt	NIG	Niger	WAG	Gambia
		NL	Netherlands	WAL	Sierra Leone
F	France (including	NZ	New Zealand	WAN	Nigeria
	overseas			WD	Dominica
	departments and	P	Portugal (including	WG	Grenada
	territories)		overseas territories)	WL	St Lucia
FJI	Fiji	PA	Panama	WS	Western Samoa
FL	Liechtenstein	PAK	Pakistan	WV	St Vincent
		PE	Peru		
GB	Great Britain	PL	Poland	YU	Yugoslavia
GBA	Alderney ⎫	PY	Paraguay	YV	Venezuela
GBG	Guernsey ⎬ Channel				
GBJ	Jersey ⎭ Islands	R	Romania	Z	Zambia
GBM	Isle of Man	RA	Argentina	ZA	South Africa
GBZ	Gibraltar	RB	Botswana	ZR	Zaire

BENEATH THE SEA

The undersea world is sometimes called 'inner space', or the world's last frontier. At the moment the number of people in the world goes up by two every second. This means that there are around 173,000 more people to feed, clothe and provide for today than there were yesterday. Tomorrow there will be another 173,000—and so on. If this continues we will eventually run out of living space.

Some experts think the answer may be to start living under the sea. Already supplies of fuel and raw materials are running low on land, and we are having to harvest the vast riches of the sea. The picture on the previous page shows one of the many machines used for working under the ocean.

The top picture (right) is of an ocean city of the future. It surrounds a calm lagoon, used for small boats and recreation. Living accommodation would be built into the walls, going down into the sunlit upper layers of the sea. Such a city might be tried out as a holiday resort. The bottom picture shows an 'undersea habitat'—a home and laboratory where scientists and divers can live and work for weeks or months on end. Unlike the ocean city, such undersea habitats have already been built.

Living Down Below

Working and living beneath the sea poses similar problems to working in space, although the sea is rather less hostile. The two main problems are the great pressure deep below the surface, and the lack of air. Today divers carry their air supply in an aqualung on their back. In an undersea habitat such as Sealab, air can be piped down from a 'mother ship' above, or it may be carried on board in

cylinders. But it cannot be ordinary air.

Living and working at great depths, the divers are at the same pressure as the water around them. When we breathe, our blood absorbs oxygen from the air. Breathing air at a very high pressure, a diver's blood absorbs much more gas than usual. If he rose suddenly to the surface, this extra gas would form bubbles in his blood, causing pain, paralysis and even death. This is called decompression sickness, or the 'bends'. Also, if a diver breathed normal air, the extra oxygen absorbed by his blood would make him feel drunk. To avoid this he must breathe a special mixture of gases. And to avoid the bends, he must rise to the surface very slowly. This gives his body time to get rid of the gases. Another way is to seal the diver in a decompression chamber. Inside this, he can relax in comfort as the pressure is slowly reduced.

A Fishy Future

There is in fact plenty of oxygen dissolved in sea water. Fish have gills so that they can breathe this oxygen. Human beings do not. But scientists are working on ways which may enable us to breathe like fish. They have found that new materials called polymers can keep out water but let in oxygen. Perhaps in the future we will be at home underwater, breathing through polymer bags.

In an undersea city the houses and other buildings would all be completely sealed. Inside, the pressure and the air would be what we are used to—just as they are inside submarines and submersibles. Fresh air from above the sea could be piped down, or it could be extracted from the sea water, as is done in some submarines. In that case the underwater city would be independent from the surface world above.

ROBOTS AT HOME

Already many homes have robot-like machines to make our lives easier. Some control washing machines and central heating. Others are inside pocket calculators and cameras. In the future we may have robot servants to do almost all the jobs in the home and garden.

These servants would be controlled by an electronic brain or computer, which could be stored in the attic and which would run all the robots electronically. The brain would control vacuum cleaners, lawn mowers, food mixers, cookers and other gadgets.

We would be able to give the brain its orders, telling it what jobs to do and when to do them. If we forgot about jobs that needed doing, or

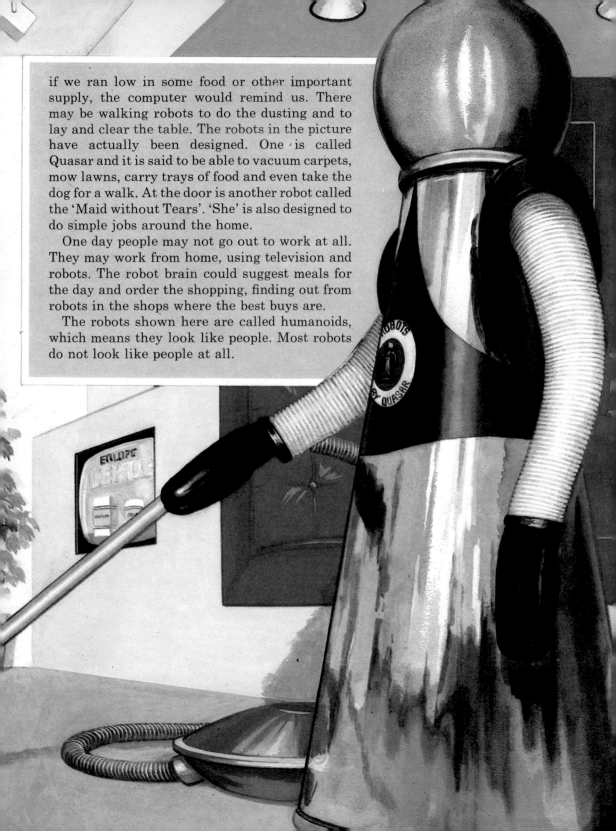

if we ran low in some food or other important supply, the computer would remind us. There may be walking robots to do the dusting and to lay and clear the table. The robots in the picture have actually been designed. One is called Quasar and it is said to be able to vacuum carpets, mow lawns, carry trays of food and even take the dog for a walk. At the door is another robot called the 'Maid without Tears'. 'She' is also designed to do simple jobs around the home.

One day people may not go out to work at all. They may work from home, using television and robots. The robot brain could suggest meals for the day and order the shopping, finding out from robots in the shops where the best buys are.

The robots shown here are called humanoids, which means they look like people. Most robots do not look like people at all.

ENERGY FOR TOMORROW

Most of our energy comes from the Sun. Coal, oil and gas—the fossil fuels—were formed from plants and animals which depended for their life on the Sun's warmth and light. Scientists and engineers are now experimenting with ways of using the Sun's heat directly. If they succeed, we need never be short of energy. Already homes in some parts of the world use solar energy to heat their hot water. Solar panels on the roof soak up the Sun's heat and pass it to water flowing through pipes in the solar panel.

A more advanced method is to use masses of mirrors. These collect sunlight from a large area and shine it onto a 'solar boiler'. Steam from the boiler can then be used to drive electricity generators. Solar cells are yet more advanced. They turn the Sun's heat directly into electricity. At the moment they are very expensive and are used mainly in spacecraft. But in tomorrow's world they may power our cars and other forms of transport. And giant arrays of solar cells out in space could provide much of the world's electricity.

Wind Power
The wind is another form of natural energy which will never run out. Wind power has been tapped for nearly 2000 years, since men first built windmills to help them pump water and grind corn. Today modern windmills can convert this force into electrical energy. Many designs are being tried. One is shown in the small picture (far right). Called a Darrieus windmill, it is shaped like a whisk, and catches wind from any direction.

When the wind is blowing, the electricity generated by this mill can supply several homes. In parts of the world with fairly steady and constant winds, chains of windmills could supply all the electricity needed.

Water Power
Water has also been used as a source of energy for a long time, at first to turn simple water wheels, and more recently to generate hydro-electricity. But we are only just beginning to learn how to tap the vast energy in the oceans. The Rance tidal power station in France is a new scheme which uses the force of the tide to generate electricity. It is rather like a dam built across an estuary. As the tidal water surges

through, it turns the turbines.

Using the energy of waves is more difficult, but engineers have designed several possibilities. One is shown in the large picture. A row of giant floats ripple up and down in the waves. The rocking movement is used to make electricity.

Thermal Power

Another idea, the thermal power station, makes use of the difference in temperature between warm surface waters of the sea and the much colder water deep down. The warmth of the surface water is enough to boil ammonia, to turn it to gas. This gas could be used to drive turbines. The gas is then cooled by the cold water from deep below, and turned back to liquid.

LIVING IN SPACE

As the Earth runs short of room and raw materials, people may start living in space. The illustrations show what a space colony of the future might look like. You can see Earth in the distance at the bottom of the picture. Each space station in the colony is rather like a gigantic spacecraft. Inside it there would be towns and villages, fields, farms and factories. The station would spin like Earth to produce a force like gravity. Materials needed to build the colony could be mined on the Moon.

The Sun is always shining in space. Its heat and light would be used to generate electricity, and to grow crops. Hinged mirrors would shine the sunlight down onto the land inside, or cut it off, to give day and night. Some crops could be grown in special pods outside the main structure. Inside each pod the climate would be made to suit the crop exactly. Noisy or dirty factories could also be in pods, so that the actual living areas would be quieter and cleaner than on Earth. There would be plenty of room for all sorts of sports and games. There could even be a low gravity area in the colony for new 'space sports'.

Transport between colonies would be fast and cheap, as there is neither air nor gravity in space to slow craft down. For journeys to Earth, colonists could travel in space shuttles.

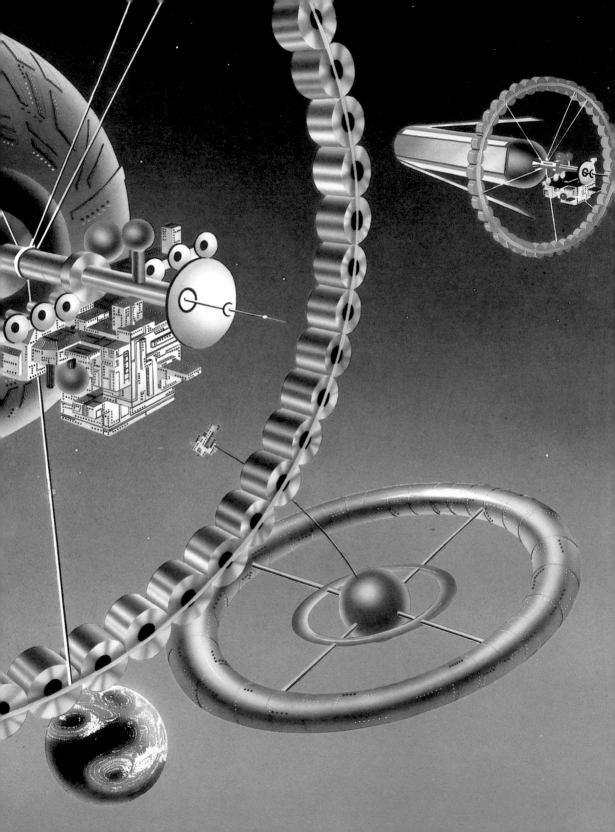

LIFE IN OUTER SPACE

There are countless millions of stars in the Universe, and many must have planets orbiting them. Many astronomers think there must be life on some of them. They listen for radio messages and send messages from Earth, hoping to make contact. The problems are enormous. Aliens from another world would not speak our language. And the distances are so vast that a radio message takes four years to reach the nearest star.

Many people think that aliens have been visiting Earth for some time—in UFOs. A UFO is an Unidentified Flying Object. The pictures show the three main kinds of UFO sightings or encounters. In a close encounter of the

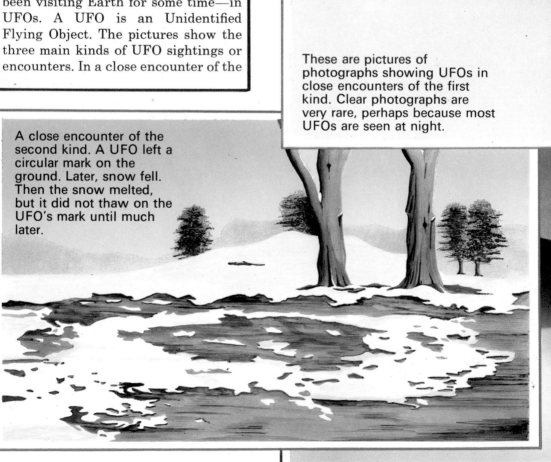

These are pictures of photographs showing UFOs in close encounters of the first kind. Clear photographs are very rare, perhaps because most UFOs are seen at night.

A close encounter of the second kind. A UFO left a circular mark on the ground. Later, snow fell. Then the snow melted, but it did not thaw on the UFO's mark until much later.

first kind, a UFO flies fairly close but does not land. In one of the second kind, the UFO leaves some physical traces. In a close encounter of the third kind living creatures are seen in or near the UFO.

UFOs may be dreams, or they may be craft from outer space. If UFOs are spacecraft they must travel much faster than Earth scientists think possible. Or they must travel in ways we do not understand. Some people think UFOs may be time travel machines, or that they come from universes around us which we cannot see. This would explain why there are so many reports of UFOs suddenly vanishing into thin air. Perhaps there are all sorts of forces and dimensions that we have not yet discovered.

A close encounter of the third kind. Many witnesses have described the 'ufonauts' (UFO occupants) they say they have seen. These are often like small human beings but with large heads.

Facts & Figures

CAPACITY

Metric Units
millilitre (ml)
1,000 ml = 1 litre (l)
100 l = 1 hectolitre (hl)

Imperial Units
gill
4 gills = 1 pint
2 pints = 1 quart
4 quarts = 1 gallon = 277.274 in^3

INTERNATIONAL PAPER SIZES

A0 841 × 1,189 mm
A1 594 × 841 mm
A2 420 × 594 mm
A3 297 × 420 mm
A4 210 × 297 mm
A5 148 × 210 mm
A6 105 × 148 mm
A7 74 × 105 mm

WEIGHT

Metric Units
milligramme (mg)
1,000 mg = 1 gramme (g)
1,000 g = 1 kilogramme (kg)
100 kg = 1 quintal (q)
1,000 kg = 1 metric ton, or tonne (t)

Imperial Units
dram (dr)
16 dr = 1 ounce (oz)
16 oz = 1 pound (lb)
14 lb = 1 stone
28 lb = 1 quarter
112 lb = 1 hundredweight (cwt)
20 cwt = 1 ton = 2,240 lb

AREA

Metric Units
square millimetre (mm^2)
100 mm^2 = 1 square centimetre (cm^2)
10,000 cm^2 = 1 square metre (m^2)
100 m^2 = 1 are (a) = 1 square decametre
100 a = 1 hectare (ha) = 1 square hectometre
100 ha = 1 square kilometre (km^2)

Imperial Units
square inch (in^2)
144 in^2 = 1 square foot (ft^2)
9 ft^2 = 1 square yard (yd^2)
4,840 yd^2 = 1 acre
640 acres = 1 square mile (mile^2)

VOLUME

Metric Units
cubic millimetre (mm^3)
1,000 mm^3 = 1 cubic centimetre (cm^3)
1,000 cm^3 = 1 cubic decimetre (dm^3) = 1 litre
1,000 dm^3 = 1 cubic metre (m^3)
1,000,000,000 m^3 = 1 cubic kilometre (km^3)

Imperial Units
cubic inch (in^3)
1,728 in^3 = 1 cubic foot (ft^3)
27 ft^3 = 1 cubic yard (yd^3)
5,451,776,000 yd^3 = 1 cubic mile (mile^3)

ANGLE

second (")
60" = 1 minute (')
60' = 1 degree (°)
90° = 1 quadrant, or right-angle
4 quadrants = 1 circle = 360°
1 radian = 57.2958° = 57°17'44.8"
2n radians = 1 circle = 360°
1° = 0.017453 radian

LENGTH

Metric Units
millimetre (mm)
10 mm = 1 centimetre (cm)
100 cm = 1 metre (m)
1,000 m = 1 kilometre (km)
Imperial Units
inch (in)
12 in = 1 foot (ft)
3 ft = 1 yard (yd)
1,760 yd = 1 mile = 5,280 ft

NAUTICAL MEASUREMENT

1 fathom = 6 feet
1 nautical mile (old) = 6,080 feet)
1 nautical mile (international) =
   1.151 statute mile (= 1,852
   metres)
60 nautical miles = 1 degree
3 nautical miles = 1 league
   (nautical)
1 knot = 1 nautical mile per hour

CONVERSION FACTORS

1 acre = 0.4047 hectares
1 centimetre = 0.3937 inch
1 cubic centimetre = 0.0610 cubic
   inch
1 cubic decimetre = 61.024 cubic
   inches
1 cubic foot = 0.0283 cubic metre
1 cubic inch = 16.387 cubic
   centimetres
1 cubic metre = 35.3146 cubic feet
          = 1.3079 cubic yards
1 cubic yard = 0.7646 cubic metre
1 foot = 0.3048 metre = 30.48
   centimetres
1 foot per second = 0.6818 mph =
   1.097 km/h
1 gallon (imperial) = 4.5461 litres
1 gill = 0.142 litre
1 gramme = 0.0353 ounce =
   0.002205 pound
1 hectare = 2.4710 acres
1 hundredweight = 50.80
   kilogrammes
1 inch = 2.54 centimetres
1 kilogramme = 2.2046 pounds
1 kilometre = 0.6214 mile =
   1,093.6 yards
1 litre = 0.22 gallon (imperial)
        = 1.7598 pints (imperial)
        = 0.8799 quarts

1 metre = 39,3701 in = 3,2808 ft
                    = 1.0936 yd
1 mil = 25.4 micrometres
1 mile (statute) = 1.6093 kilometres
1 mile (nautical) = 1.852 kilometres
1 millimetre = 0.03937 inch
1 ounce = 28.350 grammes
1 pint (imperial) = 0.5683 litre
1 pound = 0.4536 kilogramme
1 quart (imperial) = 1.1365 litres
1 quarter = 12.70 kilogrammes
1 square centimetre = 0.1550
   square inch
1 square foot = 0.0929 square metre
1 square inch = 6.4516 square
   centimetres
1 square kilometre = 0.3860 square
   mile
1 square metre = 10.7639 square
                    feet
                = 1.1960 square
                    yards
1 square mile = 2.5900 square
   kilometres
1 square yard = 0.8361 square
   metre
1 stone = 6.350 kilogrammes
1 yard = 0.9144 metre

PRINCIPAL LANGUAGES

Mandarin	500 million speakers in north and east central China.
English	320 million in the UK and Commonwealth, Ireland, South Africa and USA.
Hindi	170 million speakers in north central India.
Great Russian	170 million speakers in USSR.
Spanish	140 million speakers in Spain, Central and South America.
German	100 million speakers in Germany, Switzerland and Austria.
Japanese	100 million speakers in Japan.
Bengali	90 million speakers in Bangladesh and east India.
Arabic	80 million speakers in Middle East and north Africa.
French	80 million speakers in France and Canada.
Malay/ Indonesian	80 million speakers in Malaysia and Indonesia.
Portuguese	80 million speakers in Portugal and Brazil.
Urdu	80 million speakers in Pakistan.
Italian	60 million speakers in Italy.
Cantonese	50 million speakers in south China.
Min	50 million speakers in south and east China.
Wu	50 million speakers in east China.
Javanese	45 million speakers in Java.
Telugu	45 million speakers in south-east India.
Ukrainian	41 million speakers in USSR.
Bihari	40 million speakers in north-east India.
Marathi	40 million speakers in west India.
Tamil	40 million speakers in south-east India and Sri Lanka.
Korean	37 million speakers in Korea.
Punjabi	35 million speakers in north India.
Polish	33 million speakers in Poland.
Turkish	28 million speakers in Turkey.

MAJOR RELIGIONS

Christians	1,000 million (585 million Roman Catholics, 325 million Protestants, 90 million Eastern Orthodox)
Jews	15 million
Moslims	500 million
Shintoists	60 million
Taoists	30 million
Confucians	300 million
Buddhists	200 million
Hindus	500 million

Index

Page numbers in *italics* refer to pictures.